In.cor.ri.gi.ble

David Alfie Languedoc

Suite 300 – 990 Fort St
Victoria, BC, Canada, V8V 3K2
www.friesenpress.com

Copyright © 2015 by David Alfie Languedoc
First Edition — 2015

ISBN
978-1-4602-5167-6 (Hardcover)
978-1-4602-5168-3 (Paperback)
978-1-4602-5169-0 (eBook)

1.Biography & Autobiography, Personal Memoirs

Distributed to the trade by The Ingram Book Company

Table of Contents

A LITTLE BOY

Lost,   un*certain*,   confused   too many people in his little world

He wonders why? *Why?*

Why?

So lonely . . ..   **All by himself**

Lonely   .   .   . By himself among strangers

Unsure   of

his   surroundings

Sad . . . . . very sad . . . . . . **Too much pain**

Fearful   of   People

and Things

ANGER TAKES CONTROL

The result is **more pain**, too much pain

He hits. . He kicks . . . . He lashes out!

Love vs. lost, lonely, sadness, fear and anger   leading to *self-destruction*

Love is stronger . . . . Patient . . . . More powerful . . . . Flexible

A man . . . struggles . . . Releases

Lets love in

Author:
David Languedoc
Thunder Voice

What
It
Was
Like

The Wellesey Hospital

As I regain consciousness, as I have many times in my short fourteen years in this world, I feel extremely scared, disorientated, alone, and an incredible sense of shame and remorse. I have a feeling of Déjà Vu; you know that feeling that I have been here before. I do not know where this place is. There is a pounding in my head, as if someone or something had pounced on it repeatedly. This headache is far worse than any I have experienced before now, and I wish that someone, anyone would end this pain. The room is still spinning, yet I feel an almost calming sensation. At least if the entire world is in constant turmoil, I know I that I must fit in somewhere, but where? The room I am in appears to be extremely bright and I am surrounded by what looks like a white curtain. I realize as I move my left hand slightly that I am hooked up to an IV machine which continues an irritating beep – pause – beep – drip – pause – beep – pause. This sound, although familiar, makes my situation even more frightening. I start to feel like I could explode with anger, smashing everything and anyone in sight. Yet I know that there are some serious consequences if I start causing another disturbance. I feel this terrible throbbing in my left hand. As I slowly raise my arm at the elbow and tilt my head up off the pillow, I see that my entire left hand is wrapped in white cloth from my mid-forearm to the tips of my fingers. "What the fuck happened!? What happened to my hand, and where the fuck am I?" I experience an overwhelming panic as I attempt to regain any ounce of self-respect I can muster. As I lay my head back on the pillow, I close my eyes and repeat to myself, as I have so many times before, "What the hell is wrong with me? Am I crazy or something? How did I get here? What did I do this time? I can't remember anything I did last night." I remember having dinner at home, but even by that time I had mixed several shots of hard liquor with several beers, and this was before I left my home. Oh, and there was that shitty red wine with dinner. Wine is a drink I would tolerate if there isn't anything else to drink, or it was free and offered with a good roast beef dinner. I had to be pretty desperate to drink wine. After dinner, what did I do? I don't even remember leaving the house. Where did I go? How the hell did I end up here? As I lay on the bed my mind is flooded with so many negative thoughts. My emotions are all over the place, from anger to shame, from fear to loneliness, from self-hate to extreme sadness, to guilt. No one emotion overpowers the others. They all consume me with the same intensity. Sometimes I would convince myself that "I would be better off D E A D, I wish I would DIE!"

This was not the first time that I had thoughts of wanting to end my life. I have been plagued with these thoughts as long as I can remember. I don't remember the first time I thought of dying, but the intense, overwhelming emotion is so powerful that it almost fills me with a sense of relief as I could just imagine what it would like to die, to not feel anything. I've heard many times that death is a real comfort. You are at peace, floating to wherever you go free of pain, chaos, and stress. No anger, no shame, no hate, and no fear. Just comfort. That's that I've heard anyway.

The room is still spinning from the booze and drugs I took the night before. Even as I try hard to squint at the light, which will often slow down the spinning sensation, I realize that I am fighting another losing battle. So I decide to just close my eyes and shut out the world, and everybody in it. Very quickly I am back into the unconscious state where I came from. Maybe when I wake up all this will be a dream. But in too short a time – maybe an hour or so – I awaken again in the very same position. This time I know where I am. I am in the Emergency room of the Wellesley Hospital in downtown Toronto. A doctor slides open the curtain and appears to be in a hurry as he approaches the left side of my bed. He looks rested, clean-shaven, neat and tidy; almost too sterile. His hands are white and so clean. I have often wondered how these professionals keep so impeccably tidy all the time. There are no signs of trauma on his white, pressed jacket as he reaches into his chest pocket to retrieve a pen with his right hand, while a clipboard is firmly grasped in his left hand, and his stethoscope hangs around his neck.

He is poised and ready as he prepares himself to give me the good and bad news. He is so matter-of-fact as he relates to me my situation. It's as if he has presented this speech a thousand times before. I know for a fact that I have heard this monologue at least a few dozen times myself.

"Hello David, my name is Doctor Pain. How are you feeling this morning?"

Silence follows. I think to myself, *"What a fucking stupid question. I feel like shit."*

"I imagine you have a few questions about how you ended up here, so let me give it to you straight."

Silence again. I think to myself, *"Great, I really don't want to hear this."*

"You were admitted here at 2:16am by the Metropolitan Toronto Police. They responded to a possible Break and Entry on Roxborough Drive in Rosedale, and found you in the middle of the street directly in front of the Roxborough address. You had a very serious laceration to your left hand. It appears you put up quite a fight as they placed you in the cruiser. The good news is that you not being charged with any crime, and that you will be released from this hospital in a short while. The bad news is you almost severed your left thumb. We have placed you on an antibiotic drip to hold off any infection. You will be discharged very soon. If there is anyone who can pick you up that would be the best scenario, or you could call a taxi."

As I lay there and processed his words, all I can think of is that I don't have any money for a taxi, and I am not going to phone home and bother my mom. As a matter of fact I'm going to have to come up with a really good story as to what happened to me – because I am not going to admit this to anyone. This is for me to know and nobody else.

"I'll be ok Doctor, I'll walk home. What time is it now?" I ask.

"It is 4:51am. We will want to change your dressing again before you are ready to go. Now David, it is imperative that you follow the directions I am about to give you, and that you follow these instructions upon your discharge from the hospital. Your left hand and thumb required twelve stitches to close the wounds. When you return home you must soak your hand three times daily and apply this ointment, wrap your hand and thumb with new gauze each time. If you follow these instructions then your hand will heal. You will have scars that will remain indefinitely, but you should have full use of your hand. If you do not do take proper care of your injury then you run the risk of a possible infection setting in, that could result in the amputation of your thumb."

I was discharged from the hospital at 5:35 am. This was not the first time I walked home at this hour in the morning from this same hospital. I cannot begin to tell you how depressing this walk was. All I could think about was how I could end all the pain and anger I felt inside. Death would be a welcome relief to the confusion and self-hatred I experienced on a daily basis. I am just over fourteen years of age and going nowhere fast. I started smoking cigarettes and inhaling airplane glue, nail polish remover, and a room deodorizer called Medi-Mist at age twelve. Alcohol soon followed, and then I immediately launched into any type of drug I could put in my system. I soon realized that none of this worked. Little did I know I would end up requiring this type of medical attention many more times before there was any hope for recovery. I had only been using substances for two years, and I knew already that I was in way over my head. However, I could not see myself trading the humiliation and turmoil that I created when I was out of it for the pain and suffering that I experienced when I was straight. Either way I was screwed. I was screwed when I used and I was screwed if I didn't. I am probably no different from other people in this world, yet at times I feel like I'm the only one who suffers. We all have different stories in life, but there are others who have similar experiences. Some of us can only remember the painful times. Even at age fourteen I could not even begin to tell anyone about the pain I felt inside. There was no one I trusted enough to let into my head and into my heart. I had lost the ability to trust others long before I started sniffing, drinking, and drugging. I had been hurt, abused, forgotten, ridiculed, and felt out of place for as long as I could remember. I have always felt lost, lonely, sad, fearful, and angry. I believed in my heart that I would always feel this way, and that I would never really experience any true joy or happiness. I was destined to live an existence in which I was powerless over all events and circumstances in my life, while at the same time feeling responsible or to blame for those same events. For a while I even believed that I was jinxed, and that at an early age I possessed the power to end lives. That's right, the power to end someone's life, just through mere association with me. In short, if you got too close to me, you would die, and it would be my fault. My earliest memory was around age three and it is a memory that will be with me for the rest of my life. It was this experience that catapulted me into a life dictated by pain and fear.

As I write this down now I often find it difficult to actually believe that I am talking about myself. Sometimes it seems as though I am talking to you about someone else; yet, I know the events, which I am about to share with you, are my own experiences. At times I have been asked if I somehow, somewhere, learned to place my experience in the third person, as a way to deal with the shock of my early childhood experiences. To some degree I believe this is true. But I have found many other ways to cushion the impact of these experiences, and some of these I hope to share with you. You see, I have somehow learned to shield myself from the impact of severe trauma. In doing so, I found a way to cope with these experiences, which would eventually backfire on me to the point that I would almost take my own life. The very thing I avoided – the pain – would ultimately destroy me. I have learned throughout my life that there is only one way to deal with pain – straight on – by facing it. Not by denying it, or by clouding it through alcohol and drugs, or by moving away from it. But by processing each and every experience I have had. My MO was to pretend, forget, and block out my experiences. My way proved almost fatal. Some of the information provided in my story is extremely vivid, and it is with the utmost level of honesty that I share this information with you. I will make a promise to you that I will not just dump my life story on you without 1) offering you some concrete ways to deal with this information, and 2) leaving you with a feeling of hope that you can actually be a better person for having read these pages.

I know that I have suppressed feelings for a very long time. I have tried desperately to block out the experiences, events, and memories in my early years. Yet I keep returning to what I refer to as "my dark place", a place where only I go when I know that something terrible is about to happen. A place that serves as a constant reminder to me that I am a mean, cruel, and uncaring person; a person who deserves the worst that this world has to offer. The only way that these repressed experiences ever surface is through periods of severe depression during which my existence in this world is unbearable. Depression is actually putting it mildly. During these periods I truly wish to be dead. I have wanted all the pain to go away, before I hurt someone else, again. I did not ask for this way of living, nor would I wish it on my worst enemy. Nonetheless, I am who I am.

I decided to share my life story with you, as a result of my many, many years of working with others in the Child Care and Social Work professions. The feedback I have received over and over again is that I should write down my life story so that others could learn from my experiences. I have shared my story with thousands of children, youth, families, college and university students, professionals, therapists, and in self-help programs; I have offered my experiences to whoever cared to listen.

I have come to understand that many of us have unresolved issues from our past and that I am not alone in this regard. However, as I walk through my journey in life I am constantly reminded that only I am responsible for my issues, and only I can face the demons in my past. It is this understanding which has brought me to a point in my life that I have decided to share my journey.

I have a message to share that I pray will assist me to bringing closure to my unresolved issues, while at the same time helping others who seek resolution to their experiences. I am hopeful that these few short pages will act as a resource to anyone who may have had similar experiences. I do believe that there are so many others who feel the way I have, and who may struggle from time to time as I have. I am also hoping that these pages can be a source of comfort to the professional community, as there are many helpers in this world who struggle to understand their clients' situation.

Finally, I offer my story to any child, teen, or parent who is lost, lonely, sad, fearful, and angry. To them I would like to say, "Everything is going to be all right."

I heard these words for the first time at the tender age of four. They meant the world to me then, and they still do to this very day. In order for you to fully comprehend the importance that these six words have for me, I need to start at the beginning. I need to take you back to a place in Southern Ontario where I was born. We need to go back to June 5, 1955, to a place that not many people are aware of; Saugeen First Nation. This is a small community in a remote part of Southern Ontario. These communities exist all over Canada and across the United States. It was at Saugeen where my story begins and it was at Saugeen where my life began. It was at this small community where I was launched into a world of chaos, pain, shame, and eventually, to several suicide attempts. In no way do I blame Saugeen for these events. In no way is any one responsible for the chain of events that were about to unfold. Life is full of scenarios that just happen.

The Indian Reservation I was born on was a broken place. It is located just a stone's throw away from Southampton, Ontario, which is a hop, skip, and a jump from the southern shores of Lake Huron. As with the entire Province of Ontario, this region is picturesque. My home reserve is called the Saugeen First Nation. It is home to several thousand Band members, consisting mostly of Ojibwa ancestry. The reserve is like most others in this country; small and unassuming. If you don't watch out carefully you are likely to drive right through the reserve without even noticing you were there. I did, the very first time I traveled there as a young adult.

Highway 21 runs directly through the reserve, dissecting the community in half. As with many other Reserves in Canada, there is a major highway which runs right through the middle of the community. This has resulted in many fatal accidents. The community members usually use these major roadways to walk from one area of the reserve to another. I know that these highways have taken many lives. I know it in a deeply personal way. I witnessed such an accident and it changed my life forever.

Life At Saugeen

I was born on June 5, 1955, on the Saugeen First Nation Indian Reserve, Southampton, Ontario. I was told that my father, James Petonoquot, also from the Saugeen Band, was eighty-six years of age when I was born. That means that my biological father was born in the year 1869, and died July 26, 1955, just one month after my birth. I do not have knowledge of where he was born. I think he must have been raised in Saugeen. When I was informed of my father's age I experienced four different reactions: 1) Why is a man so old having children? 2) I didn't know men that old could have children! 3) That's disgusting! and 4) I am one of the luckiest people in the world to even have been born!

Since this time I have had many, many other questions about my father that may never be answered. I have grown up over the years with a mixture of emotions surrounding my dad that I have struggled to understand and resolve. To this day I have never even seen a picture of him, and what I have just told you about him is all I know.

My mother, Mina Martin, was also from the community of Saugeen. She was a deaf mute who reportedly cared deeply for her children. Because of her disabilities, I communicated to her through sign language. I'm not sure if I was able to speak a native language or not, or when it was that I started to learn English.

I had eight biological brothers and sisters. Some of my siblings are twenty years older than me. As I write these words I am reminded that I have siblings in their seventies. I am also reminded that out of all those siblings, I grew up with only one, Bernard. I don't remember the youngest brother, Alvin. I was told he was adopted soon after his birth and may have moved to Niagara Falls, Ontario. I have never seen him nor talked to him to this day. I also know of two bio-sisters, Kathleen and Alice who live in Cape Crocker, Ontario. I have also been informed of one brother's death. His name was Elsworth. This is all I know about my birth family. During the period I lived at Saugeen there were three brothers living at home; Bernard 4 ½ , Alfie 3, and Alvin who was a newborn. I believe that due to my father's age I could possibly have other half siblings who are older.

This is my birth family the Petonoquots.

Saugeen was impacted by alcoholism and other addictions, which were passed from one generation to the next. Unemployment was high.

Issues of family violence and various forms of abuse were rampant. Adults fuelled their addictions while the primary care and responsibilities of raising the young were often left to the older siblings, or the grandparents. The care that the young received was minimal at best. In this community however, I have the sense of belonging that is crucial to any growing child. This is my home, my family, and a part of my history.

I believe that I experienced abuse during the first three years of my life, yet I have virtually no recall of any such events. My belief comes from my understanding of how children were cared for in the community. Although Mom tried her best to care for her three youngest sons, I don't believe that she could have shielded us from abuse at the hands of others.

By the time I was one month old, my father James had died of a heart attack. This event I do not recall, yet it had an impact on me. I often think about James and wonder what he was like. Was he tall? Was he muscular? Was he small and frail? Was he a kind man or was he strict and mean? Did he work or was he on assistance? How did the community perceive him? Was he a leader, a respected member of Saugeen? Or was he a drunk who nobody wanted to be near? Did he care about me? Did he ever hold me … cuddle me … or tell me that he loved me? Do I look like him or more like Mom? How did they meet? Was he good to her? Did they plan to have me or was I an accident? Who was Dad? I have always had a yearning to know more about the man that fathered me, and I always will. The only thing that I do know about him is that he was born in 1869 and that he was in his senior years when I was delivered into this world of uncertainty. Knowing that he was an elderly man when I was conceived has always had an impact on the person I am today. Why was he fathering children at his age? He must have known that I would grow up without a dad. He must have had some idea that his son would grow up without the influence of a father. Yet somehow I have a deep love for the man who gave me a chance at life. Also, I cannot totally shoulder the blame on Dad as it takes two to tango. My mother, Mina had her role in this. Mina, as I have said was a deaf mute born on Saugeen. I have always questioned how old she was when I was born. Did she love James? Did she willing bring me into this world knowing that I would eventually experience all this turmoil? Did she love me? Did she love Dad? What was their relationship like with each other? Was their union blessed with kindness, or was it riddled with anger and abuse? I will always have I a deep love for the woman who gave me a chance at life. But what really went on between them in late 1954? What were they thinking?

My biological parents have always been a source of loss and anguish for me over the years. Most people have a clear understanding of their roots and heritage. I did not. There has always been a void in my heart when I discuss my family and I will probably always seek answers to these questions. My mother must have struggled during my early years. She had her own limitations to cope with as well as providing care to three young boys. I have often wondered how her silent world must have been for her. Missing out on so much. Not hearing her boys play. Not being able to say the words she so desperately needed to say while grieving the loss of her husband, and still meeting the needs of three energetic boys. Life must have been complicated for her. I do believe that she did the best job of parenting that any mother could under similar circumstances.

It was in May of 1958, when my two brothers and I were walking with our mom along the main road that runs through the reserve. A vehicle came speeding by and struck my mother, killing her instantly. This is the first memory I have in my childhood.

I have a clear recollection of this event as I was holding her right hand with my left hand. I could feel the impact of the vehicle hitting her as she was ripped from my hand. It felt as though something had almost yanked my arm from its socket. I have blocked out the events that took place immediately following this accident. I recall neighbors running out to the road, screaming and crying. I felt a fear that was so great that it would take years and years of healing to come to terms with this memory. I recall the vehicle speeding off down the road. I watched reserve vehicles chase after the driver. I ran to be by my mother's side as she let out her final breath. I watched her die on the road that afternoon. The rest is blocked out of my memory. I do not recall anything from this point in my life until approximately one and a half years later.

I was told much later that the driver of this vehicle fled the scene (a hit and run), but was later apprehended, charged, and convicted of impaired driving and criminal negligence causing death. I do not know what the penalty was for his crime, whether he was sent to prison or condition- ally released into the community. What I do know is his behavior would have a profound impact on the rest of my life. Life as I knew it would be forever changed. The events that would follow my mother's death would only serve to compound the fear and despair that I had just experienced. My life would get much, much worse, before it got any better.

Memories

I know that our early memories are erased due in part to our young age, and what we may remember is different from person to person. Some of us can remember events very early in our lives while others do not. In my situation my memory starts with my mother's death. From the time of her death until the time I was roughly four years of age, my memory is almost entirely blacked out; erased. I have come to understand that trauma can have an impact on a person much like an alcoholic experiences a "black out" from excessive drinking. My early years have been characterized by long periods of black outs.

I was informed many years later that the Government of Ontario, Children's Aide Society, learned of my mother's death and traveled onto the Saugeen Reserve to assess how her three young children were being cared for. When they finally located us on the reserve they observed that no one was providing the basic care that we required. In fact we were found wandering the reserve, eating hand to mouth, dirty, and unkempt. They determined that this community could not meet the requirements needed to provide adequate care and supervision for the three Petonoquot brothers. We immediately became wards of the government on a perma- nent status (PGO) or until some point in time that we were capable of caring for ourselves (age 18). This permanent apprehension status meant that the Ontario government would have authority to place us in a suit- able home setting.

This started what was to be a long and difficult process of one foster placement after another. It was at this time of apprehension that we were tested to determine what levels we were functioning at. The results of these tests indicated that we were:

1. Dull normal functioning.
2. Incorrigible.
3. Un-bondable.
4. Unsafe around other children.
5. Violent and destructive.
6. Unable to form attachments.
7. Sexually Acting Out.
8. Bed wetting.
9. Depressed.
10. Fearful.
11. Withdrawn.
12. Not able to develop trust.

Alvin, the youngest, was adopted immediately. I have not met my little brother to this very day. They decided not to separate Bernard and I, a decision that I will forever be grateful for. During the course of the following 12 months my brother and I were in eighteen foster homes.

I have very limited recall of these 18 placements. I want to believe that these families tried to take good care of my brother and I, but I do not. I want to believe that the parents that took us in were good people but were unable to meet our needs. I want desperately to believe that we were cared for and loved, but I don't. You see, any child that experiences 18 different home situations is going to be left with emotional scars for an indefinite period of time. It is inhumane to be moved so many times in such a short time-span. I believe that I experienced very traumatic events during these placements, and there are times now that I'm so grateful for not remembering all these months and all these homes. I also believe that this period of time provides a key link to the manner in which I retreat to "my dark place" even as an adult. The memories I do have are not pleasant ones. I recall being slapped, pinched, and spanked with wooden spoons and belts. I remember being sexually abused by older children, foster siblings, and adults. I have a story that I will share with you later in this book, which describes "The Room" which I was held in during one of these placements. The details of these placements I will not print, as I do not see how this could benefit anyone. I just remember re-experiencing all forms of abuse and neglect.

The impact of negative experiences seems to have a longer lasting impact than any positive ones. Let me attempt to illustrate. A child experiences the loss of a best friend due to a recent move. There is a good chance that this child will require unconditional support and attention to process the grief that accompanies this loss. They will likely progress beyond the impact of this event and be able to move forward in a healthy direction. He or she will be able to form attachments with other children, and the potential is very good that this child will eventually have a new best friend. But when all is said and done this individual will not forget the impact that this loss had on them. This child will need emotional support, encouragement, a sense of being loved, non-judgmental permission to experience their grief, a sense of security, and validation.

During my placements in Foster Care I did not experience any of these characteristics. I experienced the opposite. This was a critical developmental period (age 3 to 4 1/2) in my life. A period when most children feel loved, accepted, cared for, heard, and nurtured. It is a time for little ones to fall down and get scrapes. It is a time to learn to ride a bike for the first time and experience the warmth of a parent's hug. When independence starts to develop and the child has already established a sense of belonging in this world. They will ask questions and challenge the world as they see it. A time for learning how to separate from external needs and the creation of internal controls, to accept new challenges that life has to offer. A time when an infant transitions into childhood, shaping the young man or woman they have the potential to be one day. But this was a period in my life where I felt lost, lonely, sad, fearful, and angry.

I do not have any pleasant memories from this time in my life. All I remember is living in a world of anger, fear, and pain.

These early years have affected all aspects of my wellbeing including:

– Self-esteem	– Identity	– Trust
– Sleep habits	– Relationships	– Affect / emotions
– Ability to concentrate	– Attachment to others	– Safety
– Purpose		

All these experiences, and likely many more, have influenced the course my life has taken. I have heard countless times that the first five years of a person's life have a direct impact on how that individual will function later in life. If this is true then my ability to function in this world was drastically impaired. When most children were developing personal identity I was learning to not trust anyone in my world. While other children were being tucked into bed at night, I was experiencing 18 different homes, sets of parents, communities, and families. My ability to trust, feel safe, and to feel a sense of belonging was seriously destroyed by these numerous placements. I withdrew deeper and deeper into myself. I had thoughts that were too much for me to comprehend. The constant fear and rejection would have a life-long impact on my capacity to love, care and connect with others in this crazy world. I understood what hate meant, and vowed revenge.

There was one home that had me sleep in a small room in the basement, all alone.

I have had reoccurring nightmares about this room, and I have come to believe that the adults in this home should never have been entrusted to be Foster Parents. This is the only experience I will share with the reader from all of these placements. It will do no one any good to go into all the numerous details. It was in this room that I lost myself. It was the countless hours left alone that damaged my sense of self-worth. I felt more fear in this isolated room, and all I had was my own mind to figure things out. If ever I could define death it was in this room. I didn't think I would ever leave this room alive.

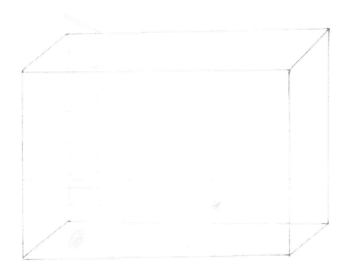

The Room

My mattress is located on the floor of my 6 x 6 bedroom, the door to which is locked for the night. The only exit from this room is a ladder that is attached to the wall in the corner of the room. At the top of the ladder is a trapdoor that opens to a room upstairs that allows me access to a toilet when I wake up in the middle to the night with the urgent need to pee. I know that if I do not make it to the bathroom that I will wet my bed, again. Besides the personal embarrassment I will experience, there will be severe consequences for my behavior. This particular night is different than most as I find my way to the toilet in time. On most nights however I would dream that I made it to the bathroom only to awake to find myself in a urine-soaked bed. The consequences I experienced usually involved physical abuse at the hands of the foster parents. These incidents were terror-filled and humiliating. I didn't know whether to fight back or yell and scream. Usually I did neither, opting to just take the beating as quietly as humanly possible. Sometimes my brain felt like it would explode in anger. I often wished that I were older, bigger, and stronger so I could turn all that pent up anger out on those adults who hurt me. One day I'll get even, or so I thought. One day I would come back and kill them. I would do worse things to them than they could ever do to me. I would cut them with a knife, and even burn them. I would tie them up and hang them from the roof by their necks. I would hurt them so bad that they could not hurt anyone else.

As I write this down I am aware of the fear that I am experiencing. I have so many questions about these people who cared for me. I wondered where was my brother was? Was he in this home too? Where did he sleep? Why did he not stop them from hurting me? Did he get similar treatment? Where was he? Why did I have to live here? Why?... Why? ... Why?

I would continue to wet the bed until the age of 11 or 12. I had several embarrassing experiences even as an adult where I would wet the bed; the last experience I recall was at age 38.

No child should ever be exposed to this way of living! No child deserves this kind of treatment! I have come to understand that following the collapse of these eighteen foster placements, my brother and I were deemed unplaceable. There was not another foster home in Ontario that would take us in. The Ontario Government could not locate an adequate home setting for the two Petonoquot brothers. All placements were exhausted. With our track record, no family in their right mind would have us in their home. The government had run out of any possible placements for the two of us. If they separated us there might have been other homes available, but the decision was made to keep us together. I had previously mentioned that I was forever grateful that they kept us together. I would much prefer to be with my brother than apart from him. He was the only connection I had to my family. Yet our union was a mixed blessing for me. You see my brother also abused me for many years. I loved and feared my brother. He protected me at times and then he would beat me senseless other times. He could be the kindest brother in the world, or the meanest. This ambivalence I had toward my brother would remain in place for years to come. Even now I ask myself many times how I feel toward him. Depending on that particular day I could love or hate him.

The Orphanage

The Children's Aide Society placed both of us at an orphanage somewhere in southern Ontario. I have never known the name of this place, but I was later told it was near Walkerton, ON. I do have vivid memories of this place, memories that I have tried unsuccessfully to erase from my mind over the years. These memories create immediate fear and anger throughout my entire body. Not only did I endure more abuse at the hands of children and adults alike, I felt trapped and helpless to do anything about it. This building warehoused roughly 65 children of various ages. Most of us were young, and almost all of us were Aboriginal. During my stay here I was subjected to abuse in all forms, physical, sexual, emotional, and mental. I witnessed other children receiving similar treatment. I was virtually stripped of every ounce of decency I had left. I was reduced to a crying, bed-wetting, starved little kid. I became a malnourished, hopeless, powerless, lost, sad, lonely, fearful, and angry little child. These experiences would ultimately shape the young man and adult I that would grow to become. I would learn very quickly that this world was a terrifying place to live. I would spend every waking moment in fear of abuse and every sleeping moment having nightmares about the abuse.

I learned to take on responsibility for other children's behavior, often being the scapegoat for them by taking the punishment for their actions. I cried every day that I lived there, and wet the bed every night. I was abused by anyone who was bigger than I was, and at age four I was the youngest. I lived in world ruled by fear, abuse, and intimidation. Even the people who were there to take care of us beat and abused us. It was a dog-eat-dog existence. The stronger prevailed, while the smallest were brutalized.

I believe that the most damaging impact of this experience was how I internalized this trauma. I was left with the impression that I would never have control/power/say over my life. I believed that I was powerless over my surroundings, my actions, and my feelings. I learned to perpetuate my own abuse through my actions with others. I learned that someone had to pay for the actions toward others. I learned to mistrust all people, young and old. I was denied food to the point that I became malnourished. My face and body were infected with sores and warts, my hair matted and lice-infected. I had lost all hope that life would be any different for my brother and me. I lived in constant fear of everyone around me. I feared the older children who not only beat each other but loved to intimidate and abuse the younger ones. I especially feared the adults. They treated me in the most inhumane ways, hitting me, sexually touching me, demanding that I gratify their perverted sexual needs, at times orchestrating group sexual activities, not to mention physically throwing children around; down stairwells etc. These care-providers were animals. I desperately wanted to kill them all.

I have many clear memories of this orphanage. I remember the front foyer of this three-story structure. The front steps (six) that lead to the front door were made of stone. The front door was huge and curved at the top. It was unlike the conventional rectangular shaped door. I remember trying with all my strength to open the front door. It was nearly impossible. But I managed to pull the door open by grabbing onto the long door handle with both hands and wedging my tiny little body in the door. I thought for a second that this door would take the life out of me. Time stood still for what seemed an eternity. I stood there trapped by the weight of this door pinned against my chest. I could not believe how thick this door was. I'm sure now it had to be four inches thick. My little brain could not comprehend why a door needed to be so big. I believed that it was probably this way so we could not get out. Time seemed to last forever. I stood trapped in the doorway hypnotized by its sheer size. I managed to get in the front door and I was immediately struck by the emptiness of the front foyer. It was completely bare of any furnishings, pictures, and even carpeting. The only item that was in this entrance was a huge wooden podium or lectern. I carefully approached it and I was instantly struck by the size of this structure. I was also extremely puzzled by its use. What was it doing there? There must be some reason for this piece of wood to be in the front hallway. After a closer inspection I noticed that this podium had some amazing markings and lettering on it. I do not know what meaning it held yet it definitely caught my attention. To give you a better understanding of this size of this structure, I quickly realized that I could hold on to the top of it and swing back and forth. Yes, it was big enough to carry my weight. I always wondered why this single piece of furniture was placed in the front entrance of the orphanage. It seemed so out of place to me. I could not explain what it was or why it stood there. It reminded me of myself, so insignificant in comparison to the larger foyer. What purpose did it have? How did it get there? What was it used for?

Another vivid memory of this orphanage was the back yard. On one occasion I was able to slip out the rear door of the orphanage and find my way to the yard. I stood for what seemed like an eternity staring at the biggest white fence I had ever seen. I mean this fence had to have been twelve feet high. I had never in my life seen such a huge fence. Where I came from there were no fences at all. Especially like this one. Another peculiar thing about this yard was the fact that the entire area was concrete. There wasn't a single blade of grass in the entire yard. I had never seen concrete to this day and it seemed really out of place in the back yard. The neighborhood I came from was all dirt roads and open yards and fields. You could go anywhere you wanted. It became very apparent to me that I would not be leaving this yard. In the far right corner of the yard was the only tree. As I sat down on the back step I was puzzled as to how this tree could grow through the concrete. I looked at the bottom of this tree to see that they had somehow cut a round circle through the concrete and there was the only dirt in the whole yard. I studied the tree more closely and I realized that the first branch of this tree pointed straight out directly over the fence. Maybe if I ran over to the tree, climbed to that branch, and hand-over-hand, I could shimmy myself into position just on the outside of the fence and drop off over the other side. Then a thought came to me that I will never forget: "I could be free!" I abruptly dismissed these plans for three reasons 1) I would have to leave my brother here, 2) If he ever caught up to me I was dead, and 3) I would probably break my leg falling.

Just as quickly however I realized that I would not be able to climb the tree, even if I wanted to. The tree was too skinny, and if I did manage to drop off the other side of the fence I would surely break my leg in the process. I sat down on the step that led down from the back door and let out a huge sigh. I said to myself two things that have stayed with me ever since: "I'm trapped" and "There's nothing I can do about it". I resigned myself to the fact that I would never have any say in what happed to me in this world. This feeling of being trapped, or powerless has been with me since my childhood days. The feeling of powerlessness has never left me. I have always struggled with taking ownership of my life, my future, my emotions, and my actions.

My memory has blocked out periods of time until I reached four and a half. All I recall feeling during my stay in this orphanage was panic and fear. I did not believe that I would ever leave this place. I was sure that I might even die in this building. I was sure that it was a matter of time before I would be either beaten or starved to death. I wasn't sure from day-to-day whether I would survive the night to wake up to the next morning. And I wasn't sure who would be abusing me next; one of the other boys, or possibly one of the adults.

All I was sure of was that my entire body ached from head to toe, inside and out. I hurt everywhere. My head raced with terrifying thoughts of death. My stomach ached with hunger. The sores on my body were open and infected. I wanted my life to end. My head kept humming inside. I could feel the pulse in my ears. My heart felt as if it would leap from my chest. I trembled most of the time and smelt like urine all the time. I do not remember bathing. I was a malnourished, skinny, little kid who cried most of the time. If someone had said to me that I was going to be ok, I know I would not have believed them.

It was going to take a miracle for me to come out of this existence. At this time in my world I did not know about, or believe in miracles. I was resolved to the fact that my life would always be this way. I did not have any belief system outside my day-to-day survival mode. I did not have even the slightest concept about faith, belief, or God. I was too young and battered to have time for make-believe. In my world, the strongest survived. The rules were dictated by the stronger. The weakest pleased the strongest. You lived like a pack of wild animals, scrounging what you could, stealing to survive, and preying on the weaker. I wish there was something positive I could say about this place, but there isn't. A person you will meet later in this book describes this place as "hell on earth." A person entering this building would experience nothing but pain and despair.

I find it overwhelming at times to recount my experiences of the orphanage. I am grateful that most of my memory of this time in my life is erased. It is difficult enough to relive what memories I do have. Even today, I can feel the fear and anger that welled up inside me then. It's gotten a little easier to talk about this experience, yet it is a lot harder to forget. I wish that this never happened. Boy do I wish that this never happened.

As I lay on the bed at the Wellesley Hospital, I submerge myself in these memories. I relive the desperation of my childhood and determine that one day I will die as a direct result of my memories and my emotions. I want so desperately to control or conduct myself as I see others do, yet, I sincerely believe that I will never be able to. I want so much for the pain to stop. I desire so much to live a healthy lifestyle, free of any mind-altering drugs. I dreamed and wished that I was not who I was. I often wanted to be someone else. Anyone else. I felt trapped in my own mind and body. I felt a constant battle between my thoughts, feelings, and actions. And most of the time I wasn't really sure who was in control. Did my feelings cause me to act or react? Or did my mind decide what was best for me? This battle raged inside me for what seemed an eternity.

The depression was overwhelming. The suppressed anger and pain were too much to handle. This is why I really believed that death would end all this pain. I was sure that death was my only option. But even as immense that the pain was I wasn't sure of how to die. How do other people end their lives? It seemed as though I was living a slow death already. The method I chose was to shut down the pain for a short period of time. The only problem was that I could not control myself when I was shit-faced. It was getting to the point where I was fearful of getting out of it because I didn't what I would do.

The first four years of my life would dog me for the rest of my life. I would never feel safe. I would never be able to trust. Everything I touched would fall apart. There was no room for day dreaming and looking toward a bright future. There was no way out of this hellish nightmare I called me. I was stuck with me and the only way out was an early death. No doctor in the world had a cure for my illness. No medicine could help me feel well. As I have stated already it would take a miracle for me to live successfully and happily in this world. All hope was lost.

If there was anything I had learned in my first four years in life it was this world sucked big time. This world was full of violent, uncaring human beings that only wanted to take their pain out on you. My only purpose on earth was to keep taking what crap this world could dish out, over and over again.

I mentioned previously that it would take a miracle to change the damage that had been done. It would take the near impossible to reverse the learning I had experienced in four short years. I do not recall how long I lived at this orphanage, but I believe it was approximately four to six months. I do remember the next events that were to unfold that would have a profound impact on my life.

Angels On Earth

Approximately two hours south of this orphanage is the big city of Toronto, Ontario. In a city with a population of a million and a half, there lived a French-Canadian family. Judy and Michael Languedoc resided in an upper-middle class, residential neighborhood called Rosedale. They were blessed with three young children, Claudette, Desmond and Michelle. This family's life was full of love, security, peace, and happiness.

Michael was a Chemical Engineer by profession and worked hard to provide for his family. Judy, who had given up a promising acting career, was a stay at home mother who provided the primary care to their three children. Each summer they would vacation at various locations in southern Ontario, and this particular summer was no exception. This summer, however would be unlike any summer they would experience.

While visiting one of their favorite resorts, Billy Bear Lodge in Huntsville, Ontario, they experienced a tragic event that would impact their world forever. Little Desmond, while fishing off the dock, slipped into the water. Claudette was the first to reach the dock only to see his lifeless body at the bottom of the lake. Although the water was shallow off the dock, it was deep enough to stop Desmond from breathing. Judy noticed that Desmond was missing and immediately dove into the lake, She was able to retrieve his little body, yet was unsuccessful in reviving him. Within the minutes it took for this accident to occur, this family was cast into a world of grief and loss. The family unit would be altered for a lifetime and because of that they would have to rely on the emotional support of each other to cope with this tragedy.

Michael, Judy, Claudette and Michelle were instantaneously thrust into a world of grief. It was during this period of grief that this couple made the decision to adopt one Native child. Their decision still baffles me to this day. It is incredible to me that they were able to find in themselves the ability to reach out to others, while in the midst of their own pain. Why Native? Well I'm sure that they were touched by the plight of Native people and felt they had what it took to provide a safe, nurturing home for someone who was less-fortunate. This ability to care un-conditionally for others, especially in the midst of one's own grief is concrete proof that they are "angels on earth". The ability to share their home, culture, values, family, and way of life is a gift that defies explanation. I have come to understand that there are many angels on earth who tirelessly give to others. Judy and Michael reached deep within themselves, and as a couple they decided to locate the right child for their home. Their search brought them to the orphanage in the fall of 1959. They phoned the orphanage and made necessary arrangements to visit. The sole purpose of this visit was to view potential children, with the intention of adopting one Native child. One. This is what took place that fall afternoon.

: The Meeting :

Judy explains:

"We drove to the orphanage, and arrived at the agreed upon time. We walked up to the front doors and proceeded to open them. I felt as if I had opened the doors to hell. All I could hear were children's cries and I could feel the pain that blew past me as I stood in the front doorway. I could not believe that this place provided care for children. I never want to experience that again! After a long, long wait, this old, heavy looking woman came into the foyer, and in a loud booming voice she said,

"'Who are you, and what do you want?'"

Judy goes on to say:

"I was nearly knocked off my feet with the manner in which this woman greeted us. I could not believe that she was the one who was in charge. 'We are the Languedoc's and we made an appointment to meet some children. We are interested in adopting a native child'.

"'A Native child eh! Well let me see what we can do,' the manager said. She walked over to the middle of the foyer stood the stopped at the podium that I used to swing on."

Judy goes on to say:

"The manager walked up to this podium, opened a binder which had information about every child in the orphanage, and started to thumb through it as if it was a shopping catalogue."

"'Well let's see . . . you don't what this child. No this one's too old. Not this one either. And certainly not these two, they're incorrigible!'

"'What did you say?'

"'You don't want these two, they're real bad, there's no hope for them!' the manager repeated."

"'I beg your pardon, **I DON'T BELIEVE ANY CHILD IS INCORRIGIBLE!** I want to see them both!'

"'Well . . . . . ok. If you say so . . . uh... I'll go get them."

As I write this down I thought I would attach a definition of the word incorrigible.

"1. Bad beyond reform, firmly fixed, not easily changed, not easily influenced, unchangeable."

The manager slipped through a set of doors leading to the area that housed the orphans. She returned a while later with the two brothers. She had them both by the scruff of the neck, attempting to avoid their kicks, screams, and spit. The boys even attempted to bite the manager's arm and as they approached the waiting couple in the foyer.

The manager said,

"This one's Alfie and this one's Bernard!"

I was there. I was about four and a half years old, but I do not recall this specific event. I often wish I could because it was one of the most important meetings in my life.

Judy explains:

"Within seconds of seeing you my heart went out to you. You looked so scared that I knew I had to remove you from this place, and the sooner the better."

Only angels on earth could make the decision that Judy and Michael made that afternoon. They started to make the arrangements to adopt both of us. That means that they would accept total care of us until we turned eighteen or until such time we could care for ourselves.

I'm not sure how long it took to formalize these arrangements; a couple of weeks at the most, but I do remember leaving that place. I remember running out of the building, flying off the six stone steps and skidding to a halt in front of the building. I saw what was the biggest car I had ever seen (it was a Ford Falcon Station Wagon, with wooden paneling on both sides). I did not know where to sit so the lady told me I could sit anywhere in the back.

I opened the rear passenger door and my brother dove into the backseat and slid over to the far side. I remember sitting on my knees and looking out the rear window, watching that building slowly disappear from sight. I said I was sitting on my knees because at this time in history you were not required to wear seat belts. I watched the orphanage disappear from sight and I was so thrilled that I turned and sat on the seat and quivered with anticipation. My thoughts raced in my head: "I don't have to go back! I don't have to go back! I never have to go back! I don't have to be hurt anymore! I'm leaving. I'm leaving, going away, far away." WACK, suddenly I felt very scared. Wait, where am I going? I don't know where I'm going! Who are these people? Where are they taking us? I'm scared, I'm scared. I don't know these people! Are they going hurt me? Are they going to lock me up in my room? What are they going to do to me? I'm so scared. The feelings I experienced have always been interchangeable. I'll flip from one emotion to another at top speed. Though I could still experience one emotion for very long periods of time, depending on the situation.

My emotions have always bounced from one to another. I could flip from fear to anger, from anger to worry, and back to fear again. Sadness would always be there, and far too much of it for me to cope with. I always felt strong emotions. Not a little feeling but big, huge, overwhelming feelings that seemed to take over. My feelings would always predict an event or outcome. Quite often these predictions were extremely accurate. They had a way of warning me that I was about to be hurt, abused, touched, invaded. My feelings seemed to consume me, to overpower me to the point of suffocation. Have you ever experienced a feeling so powerful that it seemed that it could kill you? I did not honestly believe that I would ever control how I felt. I thought eventually my feelings would overpower me. Eventually my feelings would be the cause of my death.

I sat in the back seat of their Ford Falcon Station Wagon trembling like a little leaf. It was as if I was cold, shivering out in the cold winter night without a coat on. But it was a fall afternoon. It was still very warm in southern Ontario, but I felt as if it was −25. I always thought that one day I would just tremble so much that I would just eventually fall apart, crumble into little pieces. I remember the lady "with the white hair" turned around to check on us and she must have seen me trembling.

She looked directly into my eyes and said six little words that have stayed with me ever since that scary ride,

"Everything is going to be alright."

It was the first time anybody had spoken these words to me. It was the first time anyone had realized that I needed something. It was the first time someone said that they cared for me. As I heard these words come from her lips I thought to myself, *"Lady, I believe you"*. I was not able to say this, but I thought it.

I would like to take this opportunity to express to the reader that these six words are very comforting to a young child's ears. Use them any time you can. In your home, in your work, with anyone you feel could benefit from hearing them. Look at the child directly in their eyes, and repeat these words as if you mean them.

On the ride to our new home I recall the lady with the white hair (blond) sat in the front passenger seat. The man with no hair drove. But many times during this trip they would both peek in the rear seat to reassure us both. Everytime she would turn around her smile would illuminate the car's interior. I thought for a split second, "She must be an angel. They both must be angels." And angels do not hurt you. Angels take care of you. Angels are here to protect and provide safety. They love everyone, especially children. They have been around for a long time and I am driving in a car with two of them. I don't know where I got the term angels. They both looked like something from heaven, especially the woman. She had long white hair, and a big beautiful smile and the whitest teeth I had ever seen. As I sat in the backseat of their wagon I was so tempted to reach over the front seat and flick her teeth. I could not believe they were real. I'm kind of glad I didn't touch her teeth that evening in the car. I'm sure that would not have gone over well. But I was sure that she lit up the whole interior of the car as we drove on through the early evening. A new feeling was starting to ignite inside me, a feeling of being loved.

"*You are coming to live with us at your new home,*" the lady said.

"*We thought about changing your names,*" she continued.

I have a name. It's Alfie, I thought to myself.

Judy continued, "*We have been thinking about Jacques and Andre.*"

My brother and I stared dumbfounded at her.

"*Ok,*" Judy continued, "*We also thought about David and Jeffery.*"

I immediately sat up and blurted out "*Davin*"

"*Ok then,*" Judy states, "*You'll be David, and you will be Jeffery.*"

So it turns out that my first spoken word to my new mother was my new name. This would be the starting point of my new life, and my new identity. I had really no idea of what just took place but little Alfie is now David.

We drove for what seemed an eternity, (roughly 2-3 hours) south to Toronto. This was the first time I had seen a city, and this city was huge. Even the drive through Toronto to our new home seemed to take forever. I recall all the big buildings, the cars, the lights, and so many people. I felt so small in this big place. I felt scared to be in such a huge city. I had never seen so many houses, so many different buildings, street after street, signs after signs, and lights everywhere. Stores, lights. More stores, more lights. Cars everywhere. Buildings everywhere. This new world seemed unreal to me. How could one place be so big? I could not believe how many people were in this place. I recall seeing so many different people. People that I had never seen before. Some of these people had really dark skin. There were other people who dressed really differently. I saw people walking their dogs, people shopping. There were all kinds of people doing all kinds of different things. The trip into this city created all sorts of feelings for me, but mostly I remember extreme excitement and fear. Fear of the unknown. Excited to see a totally different place. Fear that I could get lost here. Excited that things might be nice here. The trip was the most frightening part of the whole day. But there was a certain new emotion that I was experiencing; "Being with adults who cared." They talked to us all the way to our new home. Some of the discussion I really could not understand. It was as if they spoke a different language, words that I had never heard before. Facial expressions that I had never seen before. Most for the trip to Toronto is blacked-out of my memory. Shock is an amazing thing. We finally arrived at our new home. My new mom said, "You got out of the car, turned around, walked back to the car and began to examine the wood paneling attached to the outside of the car." She could not explain why I was so fascinated by this but in hindsight I probably had never seen wood stick to metal. Wood on metal – what a concept. I found out the next day that it was real wood, after tearing a chunk off and snapping it in half. My new dad was standing there and watched as I stood there with two pieces of paneling in my hands. But that was day two. The night we arrived, and after assessing the paneling on the side of the car, my new mom said I could go anywhere in the house.

It turns out that I bolted from the car and ran immediately to the second floor of the house to the room that faced the back yard. This room was eventually renovated to become our new bedroom. I am not sure why I had to go to the top of this house but this is where I ended up. The room itself was the biggest playroom I had ever seen. The entire room was set up for play. I had never, ever seen so many toys in one room in my whole life. It wasn't only stacked with toys but with games, stuffed animals, trucks, cars etc. Everywhere. I could not believe my eyes. Never had I seen so many toys in one room. There was a rocking horse and a toy box. In the middle of the room was a girl, squatting, playing with something or other. I knew she was older than I, and if she stood up she would be much taller. Beside her was a huge, metal truck with the letters L O B L A W S spelled on its sides in black paint. I do not recall exactly what transpired in the next minute or two, but my new mom said this girl and I got into a scuffle over the truck. I grabbed the truck from her and I immediately launched at her connecting directly with the top of her head. Blood was streaming from the gash I inflicted and I instinctively knew I was going to get it. This girl was my new sister, Claudette. I had been in this house less than three minutes and already I was being destructive. I did not know at the time that she was my sister, but I do know that she tried to stop me from reaching that truck. I have never been very good at sharing stuff. I always felt strongly that I had rights to just about anything. If I wanted it, all I had to do was take it. Like didn't she see me coming for the truck? What's her problem, I saw it first! Besides, trucks are for boys – not girls!

Claudette was taken to the hospital that evening to have the cut in her head stitched closed. I didn't know that this girl would be a part of my life for a long, long time. I didn't know, as that truck was sailing through the air, that I would grow to love and respect this girl. All I knew was she got in between the truck and me. All I knew was that if you wanted something in this world, you took it. If you saw something that you wanted you had to fight for it. After all, everyone else had taken so much from me without asking. They took my dad, my mom, my family, my brothers and sisters, my home, my friends and neighbors, my childhood, my sense of security. I don't ever remembering anyone asking me whether or not this was ok with me. In my world, if you wanted something you did whatever it took to get it. Beg, borrow, or steal had long since been my MO. In my world, the fittest survived. The strongest always won. The weak perished.

Clearly, there was going to be a definite period of adjustment in the Languedoc household as my brother and I settled into our new home and family in Toronto. My brother and I soon became well known in the entire neighborhood. The lady with the white hair told me years later about our first meal with our new family. It was supper.

Judy explains:

"It was customary in our home hold hands and pray before we would eat. I remember in astonishment when we all sat down for our first meal and we watched in horror as David and Jeffery did not wait for prayers but started grabbing food from the platters on the table, gorging themselves until they would throw up most of what they had eaten."

The Languedoc's were a French-Canadian family who were grounded in the Anglican faith. This was a family unit who treasured family life and conducted themselves on a foundation of mutual love and respect. They had strong family values that would be tested time and time again by my brother and I. We would require constant supervision and guidance. We continually fought with each other and would always find some trouble to get into. In a short time we were swinging on the living room drapes until they were pulled from the walls. The patience and support the Languedoc family provided would be tested over and over again.

I am sure that there must have been moments when Michael and Judy wondered what they had gotten themselves into. They could not have known what they were in for when they brought us home. I was still not sleeping throughout the night. I would usually wake up screaming from my night terrors. I wet the bed almost every night. My brother and I were constantly fighting, screaming, breaking things, and so on. We started to steal everything we could, either in the home or in the community. And to add on a new dimension, we had to be registered for Elementary School.

Dad

My dad Michael was a tall, good looking man who demonstrated a high level of patience and commitment to his family. He worked hard as a Chemical Engineer and provided very well for his family. He was a gifted musician and all-around athlete. Although his work required that he be absent from the home occasionally, he would always return home ready and more than willing to make the extra effort to spend quality time with his family. Dad, as I came to know him, was the most amazing, loving, talented, energetic, honorable, and loyal man I have ever met.

He was firm yet gentle, funny but serious. He was good with his hands, whether it called for renovations on the house, to making an amazing bunk bed for my brother and me.

He always seemed to know how to fix just about anything. He played guitar so well, and this would eventually an interest that he passed on to me. Dad was the disciplinarian in the family but even when the occasion called for a spanking (which was frequently), Dad incorporated a non-aggressive and fair approach to parenting. The spankings hurt and also confused me at the same time. I had difficulty understanding how several slaps on my butt would justify as a consequence for my behavior. I have grown to advocate a "no spanking" approach in my parenting style. I have heard that on occasion a child will respond favorably to a spanking; however, this form of discipline only caused more confusion for me as a child. Even though my dad never struck me in anger, he still struck me. I started to put some trust in this man and when he hit me it added confusion to the feelings I was developing for him. As I recall the impact of these spankings, I wonder why they stand out more for me. I know there many positive interactions with Dad, yet the negative ones stand out the most. I also understand that spanking was an acceptable form of discipline in that era, but in this day in time it can be considered abusive to strike a child. This approach, coupled with the previous abuse I had already experienced in my early years, left me with the impression that at some time or other it was ok to hit, or be hit.

The most amazing part of our new family was the bond I witnessed between my mom and dad. I watched through impressionable young eyes the way they held each other, the way that Dad was always kind and considerate toward Mom, how they worked together as a team, always supporting each other. I watched Mom look at Dad with the most amazing look that can only be described a total love and respect. She leaned on him so much and he always came through. He worked hard and played hard. He was always cheerful and humorous, the life of the party. He barely ever displayed anger, but was easy to express disappointment. He loved all of his children equally and made time for each and every one of us.

I consider myself extremely grateful for having a dad like Michael. He is the only man in this world who could have the impact on me that he did. I loved him more than I could ever express. I felt proud to be considered his son. He was everything I wanted to become. He showed me what it is to be a gentleman, and passed on to me so many teachings that I hold dear to me to this day.

Mom

Judy was the most amazing woman in the world. She accepted a challenge in 1959 when she adopted two high-needs, Aboriginal brothers and rose to the occasion time after time after time. Mom taught me the meaning of unconditional love as she based her own life on the foundation that "Love could conquer anything". She radiated love from every pore in her body, and possessed the ability to soothe any pain that I experienced. She was raised herself in a home setting that was rooted in respect and caring. Her commitment to my brother and I would be tested over and over again, and each time she would not waver in her commitment to raise the two of us. Her undying love for us would ultimately be the turning point in our lives, as we struggled to cope with the impact of our early years. I realize as I write this that I could easily dedicate an entire volume to my mother's character and teachings. I will refer to her many times throughout these pages.

I will never forget a saying she shared with me at a time in my life when I was really messed up:

"Not flesh of my flesh, nor bone of my bone,
But still miraculously my own.
Don't ever forget for a single minute,
That you didn't grow under my heart, but in it."
Author unknown

Moms words were always comforting, especially to a growing child. She had a soothing voice and would always have an answer for any situation. She was raised in a strong religious family, a faith that would one day influence my need and desire to understand the workings of faith and spirituality. I would one day reach a point in my life when I could fully comprehend Mom's connection to a Higher Power that is the source of all healing. As a little boy however, her words were confusing and distant to the ears of a broken and battered child. I could not fully accept that religion, faith, and prayer were all that important. Many times I questioned the meaning behind the words I heard through religion.

Ages 4 – 8 years

It remains a mystery to me that although the years that followed were full of countless fond events and experiences, all the memories I have are negative ones. My brother and I were the only Aboriginal children in our neighborhood. I did not meet another Aboriginal person until I was 16 years of age. I struggled in all aspects of my day-to-day life. School was very difficult, friendships were hard to make and even harder to keep. Everywhere my brother and I went, trouble followed. We wandered from one incident to another. There were many fights with schoolmates, followed by spankings at home, and more strappings at school. I was continually late for class, stealing, lying, destroying property, and generally running from one chaotic experience to another. I stole from my mother's purse, sold milk jugs at the local store for cash, hurt other children with my fists, with sticks and small lengths of chain. When I did attend school, I could not remain still long enough in class to participate in the subjects that were being taught. I always felt dumb and inadequate in comparison to the other students – less than them. I felt like I did not fit in this new world, yet I had no choice as to where I stayed. I suffered on-going ear infections, and I was a chronic bed-wetter until the age of 12. I had my thumb (and later my nose) broken by my brother during one of his regular "tune-ins". All these memories have stayed with me over the years. I felt like a failure that was incapable of attaining success in everything I did. I was angry most of the time. I lashed out all of the time. I had difficulty in school with every subject. If people would laugh at me I would hurt them outside of school. It seemed as though I would never experience success in anything I attempted to do. Somehow I managed to squeak by each grade in elementary school, and move on to the next grade. My brother was no help either, as I would follow him from one grade to the next. It was a custom of our school for each class to meet their teacher for the next year. We would all parade from one class to the next and tour our new classroom to meet our teacher. This was usually done in late June of the school year. As I entered my new grade three class, the teacher looked at me and said in a voice that all of us could hear, "So you're a Languedoc, Jeffrey's brother. Well I'll be keeping my eye on you." I felt embarrassed immediately. I would not forget his words any time soon, and as a matter of fact I would live up to and even surpass his expectations of me.

But you do what you can with what you've got. Each elementary grade was more difficult than the previous one. I ended up in the principal's office more times than I could count. The principal and I had an agreement – if I was sent to his office I was to take a seat next to his door and wait for him. They had a chair waiting there that I thought he had set up just for me. I don't remember how many times I sat in that chair waiting. Often I was guilty of being late for class, fighting, or being disruptive.

My outbursts of anger, not doing assignments, not completing homework, stealing from other students, leaving school without permission, or being rude to teachers, were almost weekly events in elementary school. Now these were things that I recall doing, yet I felt unable to control myself most of the time. I was impulsive which lead to just about any outcome, and I could not seem to connect the dots between my behavior and consequences. Nothing really made any sense to me. Nothing!

1963

Most days I was late arriving to school in the morning. Every day I would run home for lunch (home was about 15 minutes from school), and most days I was late returning from the lunch break. This particular day in the fall of 1963 I was going home for lunch. I was in grade four. As usual, I left school to run home. And as usual, I left the house to return to school a little late. I knew from previous experience that if I ran as fast as I could I might make it back to school before the afternoon bell rang. I proceeded to make a mad dash for school. As usual I did not gauge my time accordingly and was fighting a losing battle to beat afternoon bell. But I was determined to make it to school on time. I had every intention of being on time. This was a routine return trip to school and today was like any other, with one exception.

I ran to the end of my street, turned the corner, and headed up Summerhill Avenue. Two blocks west on Summerhill Avenue is a "T" intersection that connects Summerhill to Glen Road. As I approach this intersection I notice out of the corner of my eye the crosswalk guard who is usually stationed at this location to make sure that the younger children were helped crossing the street safely. I found out much later that this elderly man was a retired Police Officer who accepted his role in life to help little children be safe following his retirement.

As I ran past the intersection I was overcome with the desire to throw dry mud balls at him.

In a twisted sort of way I found pleasure in watching him shield himself from my accurate assault. Following several tosses I decided that one more mud ball and I best be on my way; that is, before I'm late for school. I reached down for the last deadly mound of dirt. I paused ever so briefly to think how handy it was to have these mud balls so readily available to me. I didn't have to make them. They were just the right size for what I needed. These huge Oak trees were so nicely trimmed around their base, and someone – I don't know who – took the time to create these beautiful, hand-sized weapons just for me. I'd sure like to meet the person who thought of this and shake their hand for saving me valuable time. I grabbed the last mud ball and launched it across the street at the guard. I instinctively knew that my last shot was deadly accurate, – a direct hit! I watched him fall to his knees after the shot hit him square in the face.

Having accomplished what I started I set out to reach the school on time. Oddly enough I was late again. I knew the routine so well by now that I went directly to "the chair" outside the principal's office. What followed was another firm reprimand and two straps on each hand. It was customary that he would then escort me to my classroom. He would politely knock on the classroom door and wait for the teacher to arrive. As I entered the class I was greeted by the disappointed glare from my homeroom teacher, and the stares and giggles from 26 fellow classmates. I took my seat at the only vacant desk in the room, planning how to get revenge against the entire class.

School was the last place I wanted to be. Afternoons were worse than the mornings. I just could not find the concentration I needed to stay focused on my work. I was often restless and disruptive. Today was no different than all the others – with one exception.

The principal returned to our class this particular afternoon. He opened the classroom door, and signaled for the teacher to meet him at the door. Within seconds the entire class was staring at me. Yes everyone could tell that they were talking about me. Following a very brief conversation between the two of them my teacher walked directly to my desk. She bent down and whispered:

"David, please put your books away and go to the office with Mr. M."

I did exactly as she requested; cleaned off my desk and walked to the door to meet the principal. As I left to the stares and giggles from the other students I briefly imagined killing all my classmates. As I walked the green mile to his office I wondered what he had in store for me today. Was he going to strap me again? Was I going to have to work from the main office this afternoon? What did he want, and why was he so quiet? All kinds of scenarios played out in my little brain.

We returned to the main office and he seated himself at his huge oak desk.

"David," he glared, *"I am dismissing you from school this afternoon. You are to go directly home where your mother is waiting for you. Do you understand these instructions?"*

"Yes, sir, I have to go straight home to see my mom," I replied.

"Yes, STRAIGHT HOME! DO NOT STOP ANYWHERE!"

Nothing else was said between us and this scared the crap out of me. Usually I have more information to go on than this. This must be real serious. I had never been dismissed from class for the whole afternoon before. I hope mom is ok. Maybe she got hurt or something. Maybe something happened to one of my brothers or sisters. I left the building with mixed emotions. On one hand I was thrilled to be out of class, but on the other I was confused and scared. I guess I would find out when I got home. I reached home to the concerned, worried expression on my mother's face. She didn't have much to say. But when she did finally speak she said those few words that I hated to hear.

"David, you are to go directly to your room and wait until your dad gets home."

I knew from many times before that when she said these words it meant three things:

1.   That she meant what she was saying,
2.   I was in serious trouble and,
3.   That I would be spanked when my dad got home.

I don't recall how I spent the rest of the afternoon but the seconds felt like minutes, and the minutes like hours. I do know that I spent the time returning to that lost, lonely, sad, fearful, and angry place. I knew I was in for it. When I spent too much time by myself, with all these bad thoughts in my head, I would often consider suicide. I really didn't know the term suicide. All I knew is that I would be better off dead. I would conjure up different ways that I could end my life. I reveled at the thought of dad coming upstairs to find me dead. I would sink into a really deep depression; self-hatred and severe loneliness would be my medication. If I thought hard enough and long enough I could feel this buzzing sensation in my brain. My pulse rate you could hear, if you listened inside my ear. The blood felt like it was pumping too hard through my veins. If I really concentrated hard enough on my body I could actually put myself to sleep. Sleep was never a pleasant alternative to the real world either. Quite often I was horrified of my dream world, a place where the pain and suffering was sometime even worse than during awake time. It always seemed so real. My sleeping dreams were at times far worse than my daydreams. My little brain could conjure up the worst, most violent images. My dreams were so real. I felt as though one day I might even die in my sleep. The violence was unbearable; the fear so intense; the images in my mind all came to real life when I slept, and usually I would awaken in a panic. I would wake up sobbing uncontrollably, and quite often I would have wet the bed. Sleep, while offering some escape often left me feeling worse in the end.

I woke up just as dad's car was pulling up in front of the house. I could hear him come in the front door. I knew that he and mom were talking about me in the living room. Then I heard his heavy footsteps coming up the stairs and down the hallway to my bedroom.

I watched my bedroom door open.

As I stated earlier Dad's approach to discipline was deliberate, carefully planned out, and purposeful. He would usually start off with some well-organized line of questions. I felt as if I really had to listen to his line of questioning. It was almost like being interrogated by a detective. He usually knew the answer to his own question, and led me on this little scenario from beginning to end. I don't know how he did this but I knew that he would always get to the truth. Maybe this was one skill you learn to become a Chemical Engineer. Wherever he picked up this technique, he had it mastered. If you lied he would re-organize his line of questioning so that it eventually lead to the truth. He wasn't angry because I know what anger looks and feels like. He didn't ever raise his voice, always speaking in a calm reassuring tone (and this didn't help my situation). His questions were never difficult or long-winded. They usually elicited a direct "yes" or "no" or a brief one-line response. Boy he was good at it, and I was screwed.

"How has your day been?"

"Ok, I guess."

"You were home for lunch today?"

"Yes!"

"Did you make back to school after lunch?"

"Yes."

"Were you late getting back to school after your lunch?"

(Long pause) I thought to myself that he is trying to trick into the truth again. Should I lie or tell the truth? If I lie, it will definitely make things worse in the end. If I tell the truth right now then he will be kinder. But I know that if I lie or tell the truth I'm still going to get a spanking. Either way I'm screwed.

"Yes I was late." (*The truth, it's got to be worth something.*)

"Why were late today?"

"I don't know. I ran as fast as I could!" (*Hoping he might hear how hard it really is for me.*)

"Did anything happen on the way back to school?"

"No!" (*Nervously; now I know that this is a lie but there is no way he would know what really happened. No way*).

"Did you stop anywhere on the way back to school?"

"No, I ran most of the way, I ran as fast as I could."

"Did you stop to throw mud balls at the crosswalk guard?"

(WHAT! How does he know that? How does he know that? Did he see me? Did the crosswalk guard call him? Did one of the neighbors see me? How does he know?)

"YYYes, but ooonly a few."

"My son, a few is three. Did you throw three mud balls at the cross-walk guard?"

"Well, I think it was more than three."

"Well David, I want you to think hard before you answer. How many more than three was it?"

"Umm, aaaabout seven or eight."

"David, so you did stop on the way back to school after lunch to throw seven or eight mud balls at the cross-walk guard?"

"Yes."

"David, we have talked about throwing things at people before. Do you remember us talking about throwing things at others?"

"Yes."

"And what have I told you about throwing things at people?"

"You said not to throw things at people." (Hoping to earn a few points.)

"That right. And there's a reason why. What is the reason?"

"Because (pause) someone could get (pause) hurt?" (More points.)

"That's exactly right. Now I don't know how many mud balls you threw at the crosswalk guard, but one of them hit him directly in the eye. He was taken to the hospital this afternoon and he is blind in that eye now!"

No! . . . No! . . . No! . .No! I didn't mean to hurt him, I didn't mean to hurt him, it was an accident, I didn't mean to . . . .

"I'm sorry ... I'm sorry, I'm SORRY!!!"

(Fade to black – retreat to dark place, do not pass go, do not collect $200.00. Go directly to dark place, and do not move a muscle. Freeze. Heart rate – accelerate. Blood pressure – through the roof. Head – start pounding! Thoughts – start racing uncontrollably. This is where I belong. This is where I will always end up. I am no good, I am mean and cruel and dangerous. I do not belong here. All I am good for is hurting people. Nobody likes me. I wish I were dead. Forget the spanking – just end my life. RIGHT NOW!)

The words I heard come from my dad's mouth that afternoon have echoed in my brain for years. The spanking I received only hurt me on the butt. But the pain I felt on the inside was unbearable. How could I do this to someone? What is wrong with me? Am I crazy or something? Why do I hurt others all the time? And in the end I feel hatred toward myself.

Then I remembered the sensation I experienced when I was throwing those mud balls. I felt powerful! I felt happy to be scaring someone else. In a sick way I felt invincible at the expense of someone else's suffering. I enjoyed hurting others at the time, but this brief pleasure would ultimately result in me feeling even worse later.

As I often did, I took refuge in my "dark place" and became embedded in an inner world of self-hate and depression. The guilt and remorse I felt stayed with me for a lifetime. I could not comprehend the severity of my actions. Nor could I begin to fully accept responsibility for my behavior. All I was left with was more concrete proof that I was a mean and destructive human being. You would think that I would learn from experiences such as this. But I did not. There was more violence and destruction to come as I continued to live in my world that was based on "hurt others before they can hurt you". I would continue to operate in this MO for years before I would ever make a serious attempt to change.

I know that the weeks that followed the incident are totally blocked from my memory. I wish I could remember if I even attempted to visit this gentleman at the hospital, or if I attempted to make an apology for my actions. The impact of this experience, the guilt and shame, would remain with me for many, many years. I retreated to my "dark place", resigned to remain there indefinitely.

The Crosswalk Guard was never again seen at his post at Summerville and Glen Road. He just quietly disappeared. A kind, and gentle old man who wouldn't hurt a fly. I will always feel sorry for how I treated him.

But life at the Languedoc home had to go on. It seemed to go from one crisis to another. To this day I am still puzzled by the impact of negative experiences as they seem to last longer than the positive ones.

I have thought long and hard about why I only recall the bad times. My memory is filled with examples like this one. My heart has always felt too heavy for my little chest. I have always hated myself since my first memory. It is really difficult, almost impossible, to not think negatively. I often wondered if I would ever think the way normal children do. I wondered if I was the only person in this world that didn't want to live. I believed that if I could I would end my life. But I really had no means to do this. I thought about jumping off the Glen Road Bridge head first, but I was petrified of heights. I thought about tying a plastic bag over my head, but I knew I would eventually just take it off, because I couldn't breathe. My ideas were few and I soon gave up on the whole notion. The only option I had was to live a miserable life, because I knew that things would never get better.

Our family had grown by this time. A younger brother had come into my life, and this placed me in a new role, and exciting one. Sean would become my new sibling, and I was cast into the role of an older brother. This was a new experience for me, and an extremely rewarding one as well. It's funny that I do not recall the birth of my new brother, yet I do have many fond memories of being the "older" brother. For the first time I slipped into a care-giving role which was a unique experience in itself. In the fall of 1963 there were now five children, ages 2 – 11years. Sean was the baby of the family. For some unexplained reason I called him "skeez-ics", and later "bibzie". I could never in a million years explain how these names came about. Sean had a very special place in my heart. He looked up to me and accepted me unconditionally. I was given the opportunity to offer him the guidance and love that I never received. This would be the starting point of my ability to get out of my own head and heart and reach out to someone else. Jeff and I continued to wreak havoc everywhere, making friends that acted as we did. And life went on.

63 Was A Real Bad Year

Just as I was starting to believe that my world would turn for the better, our family experienced the most traumatic event that any family could. Dad had received a promotion with his Engineering Company. In the fall of 1963 we were in the process of moving from Toronto to Montreal. He was traveling extensively between these two cities finalizing arrangements for the move. Our home in Toronto was sold and he had purchased a property in Montreal. I recall a visit to Montreal where we had the opportunity to see our new home. It's odd, however, that this may have been a dream.

Moving to Montreal required that Dad be absent from the home for periods of time, but we all waited with anticipation at his return. He always gave us big hugs when he returned. The family singsongs in the living room were my favorite. I did not realize until several years later just how much I studied his every move while he strummed the guitar. I do recall being seated on the living room floor and I experienced an inner excitement as I watched him play. I remember being in an almost trance-like state when he masterfully picked and chorded his guitar. I watched his every move with anticipation, and listened intently to the words he sang about a squirrel in a tree named Angus. I remember gazing up at him and repeating over and over in my head that someday I wanted to be like him. That one day I wanted what he had, that I loved him so much and that I felt so much pride that he was my dad. I'm sure that Mom especially looked forward to the comfort and support he provided upon his return. I'm not sure if other sons felt the way I did. To idolize a male figure is truly a precious gift. Dad had it all – looks, talent, strength, gentleness, humor, and kindness. He was the best father I could ever have dreamed of having. He was my hero, my mentor. He had an approach to living that I first thought was fake, but I learned to understand that it was genuine. That's it; He Was Genuine.

It was in the fall of '63, November 29th to be exact. I was eight and a half years old. I woke abruptly early in the morning to the sounds of people crying and sobbing. I instinctively knew that something terrible had happened. We never woke up in the morning like this. I climbed out of my wet sleeping bag (due to my chronic bed-wetting it was easier to wash a sleeping bag rather than change linen daily) and walked the eight or so steps to my parents' bedroom. I turned left sharply and peered cautiously into their bedroom. What I saw and heard sent me into shock.

I watched, for what seemed like hours, my mom cuddling my two sisters in her bed. Claudette was on her right, and Michelle was on her left. All three were sobbing uncontrollably. I walked in and stood at the foot of the bed for what seemed an eternity. After several minutes I heard my mom explain:

"David, your daddy was flying home late last night and the plane he was in went down in bad weather. Everyone in the plane was killed. Your daddy will not be coming home. But daddy would want us all to be brave and strong. He would want us to continue loving and supporting each other.

He is heaven with God now and that he will always be watching over us."

I immediately went into shock. My thoughts started to race through my head uncontrollably. All I could think is, "Why is she lying to me? Why would she say something like this? I don't believe her!!" My heart pounded with fear. Thoughts continued to race through my head. What's going to happen to Jeff & me? You see, when people died in my world that usually meant we would have to move. But where would we go? Another foster home, or back to the orphanage. Where would we live? Why do people around me always die? Why? Why? Why?

But, now he's gone? Just like that? How do people just die like that? What happens to you when you die? Where does your body go? Who is there to pick you up after you die, and where do they take you? I want to see my dad. I want to see his face again… I want to hear his voice and watch him smile… Why do people die? Why do I know so many people that have died? Does this happen to everyone? Does everyone lose family like I do? Or, maybe it's because of me. Maybe only people that I am close to die. Or maybe I am bad luck or something. Yeah, maybe I am jinxed or something, that if people get close to me they will die.

I walked back to my bedroom and hopped back into my urine-soaked sleeping bag. I buried myself under the covers and made four little promises to myself. These promises would dictate my life for many, many years. I never shared these promises with anyone for almost twenty years. Only I knew about them.

It was under my bedding that I promised myself four things. These promises were mine and only mine. No one else would hear them. NO ONE.

"I'm not going to cry"
"I can't get angry"
"I'm not going to trust another person for the rest of my life, especially adults!"
"I'm going to hurt others before they can hurt me!"

I experienced a sensation throughout my entire body, one that I had never experienced before in my brief life. I felt my whole insides go cold. It started at the top of my head and slowly crept through my entire body.

It traveled down my neck, across my chest and arms right to the tips of my fingers. It continued down through my stomach, hips, and the upper part of my legs, to my feet, finally reaching the tips of my toes. I felt numb throughout my entire body, an inner numbness that one might experience if they were out in the cold far too long. It was as though my entire inside was ice cold. It was if I was able to shut down my internal body temperature, and stay that way.

From this point in my life, and for many years to come, I tried keep my internal emotional temperature around zero. The only time that I would allow myself to release any internal feelings was when I was alone. No one would ever be allowed to see how much I hurt inside, how much I distrusted the human race, how lost, lonely, sad, fearful and angry I felt inside. No one would ever know the real me inside because if I let anyone know then that would mean that they would die. I would not trust another human being. … EVER!!!!

The loss of my adopted father, Michael, was devastating. I regressed into an inner world of pain, uncertainty, confusion, and anger. My every thought was pre-occupied with what he experienced as he plunged toward earth in that plane. I could feel his fear. I could hear the screams and the prayers of the other passengers. I could only begin to imagine how he must have felt during his last few moments on earth. The fear that his death created went to the very core of my existence. I trembled inside just wondering how he spent his last few moments in this world. I often imagined that he was probably reaching out to others as a source of comfort, even knowing that he was about to die. I could not comprehend what his last moments were like for him. I would much rather shut myself down, numb myself, and forget all about it. Yet I know I cannot. I know that his death had, and still does have, a resounding impact on my life.

The days, weeks and months that followed are all blocked out. I do not remember what happened. I do not recall my dad's funeral. I was in shock for months, even years, following his death. I tried to keep my body temperature at zero all the time. I continued to hurt, hit, and hate. I had given up. I didn't care anymore. If I smiled it was fake. If I cried, I was alone, and if I remembered, I went crazy.

Mom did her best to keep us grounded, a role that I would not wish on anyone. My brother and I spiraled out of control. Anger and fear became the primary emotions. We never really talked about things because it was too hard for all of us. We just did our collective best to move on as a family.

I felt almost compelled to be with my little brother more. When I was with him, somehow I felt better. When I could make him laugh, I smiled inside. When he was near I felt as if I could go on.

I think Sean was around three years old when we were up early one Saturday morning. I'm sure we ate a light breakfast and decided to go for a walk to the park. The park was at the end of our street; about a five minute walk. We probably set out by 8:00 in the morning. Now if I were the parent in this situation I might already be worrying, as I am very easily distracted and will usually go wherever my thoughts lead me (us). So we spent some time at the park and then we ventured over the Governor's Bridge to a different park. We hiked through a ravine, and into a sand pit where this company produced bricks for housing etc. At the far end of this gravel/sand pit was an old abandoned, run-down apartment building. This particular structure was about eight stories high and was never completed. It sat vacant for years. It could not be completed, for one reason or another and no one was prepared to cover the costs of having it torn down. So here we are in the basement of this extremely dangerous structure playing and exploring. We must have been there for a couple of hours before I realized that we had been gone all morning. So being the responsible "older" brother I took Sean's hand and started back home. We arrived home shortly after lunchtime. As we turned the corner at the top of our street I noticed that there were several police cars, with their lights flashing, parked right in front of our house. You see my mom started to panic when we could not be found anywhere and summoned the authorities and what started as a harmless morning walk turned into a very serious situation. In the end my brother and I were able to spend some quality time together while the rest of the world feared the worst. I loved all my brothers and sisters for unique reasons; however it was the younger siblings that brought out in me the ability to give and nurture.

I did not realize that this relationship I had with younger siblings would have such a resounding impact on me. I only knew that I had some responsibility to help them when I could. As their older brother I needed to try and be there for them. Their needs had to come before mine. This would prove to be a difficult task – to put someone else's needs before my own. This would be an issue for me for years to come. It would take some adjusting to find the balance between mine and other's needs.

In my grief, I created a fantasy that I did not share with anyone for years. If any man could survive a plane crash, it was my dad. Yeah. My dad. The rock of Gibraltar; tall, handsome, funny, strong, and smart. If any could survive a plane crash it was Dad.

This little promise or secret kept my hope alive that Dad would one day walk through the front door of our home and that I would run to him, jump into his arms. That I would have the chance to say to him, "I Love You Dad", and that everything would return to the way it was. I kept my little secret for a long time. I also had a recurring dream that reinforced my little secret. This dream repeated itself for several years, and it was my little secret. It was a secret that I wouldn't tell anyone about. Only I was supposed to know. It made feel special in a way to know something that no one else did. It made me feel almost powerful to have this information about my dad that only I had. Eventually, my little secret would occupy a great deal of my sleep time and awake time. I became so preoccupied with the thought of my dad returning home that I was trapped in my own delusion. I believed it so much that it became an obsession in my mind. Over and over again I would repeat to myself that Dad would be back soon, Dad would be back soon.

Denial is a defense that I have come to learn is a natural part of the grieving process. Denial acts to protect an individual from the full impact of the traumatic incident such as the loss of a loved one. It was the denial that helped shield me from the full impact of Dad's death, until such time that I was ready to "face the actual event". In my situation, I denied Dad's death for approximately three years, or until I was about eleven years of age. It was around my eleventh year that it finally dawned on me that Dad was not going to return home, ever. Denial has a way of surfacing while you sleep, which in my case appeared in a recurring dream I had that helped kept my hopes alive that Dad would return home.

The Dream

I am standing in the middle of a road, facing a long suspension bridge. I am frightened at first because I do not know why I am standing there, or how I got there to begin with. "Why am I here?" "Where am I?" and "How did I get here?" are questions I keep asking myself over and over again. As I look toward the bridge I feel overwhelmed by the length of the bridge. I cannot see the other side. It seems to disappear into a mist. I realize that this bridge crosses what appears to be a deep, deep gorge. I realize that I am in the mountains, at a place where I have never been before. I am dumbfounded as to why I am standing in the middle of this road staring out across this bridge. I quickly notice something approaching me from the middle of the bridge. As I squint I cannot make out what it is. As I squint harder I see that this figure walking, almost stumbling toward me. As this person starts to take shape I realize that it is a man. I squint even harder to get a clearer view of who it is. As this person gets closer I see that it is a man, dressed in what appears to be a tattered and torn grey business suit. As he inches closer I can finally recognize his facial features. He looks extremely tired, he was not shaven for some time, and he looks weak as he staggers across the bridge. Suddenly I recognize this person. "It's Dad! It's Dad! He did survive the plane crash and he's trying to get to me!!! He's alive, he's alive, he's – " Suddenly I awaken from my dream screaming. I am scared and sobbing uncontrollably. I have also wet the bed again. I am exhausted from the emotional impact of my dream. My heart is beating a millions beats per second. My chest feels as if it would explode. My hands are sweaty, and thoughts in my mind race uncontrollably. As I begin to settle down I realize that I am patting myself on the head, almost reassuringly. Almost immediately I am consumed with reassurance that Dad is still alive, and only I know this. This fantasy-like way of coping with life was very real to me. It served a very useful purpose. It helped to shield me against the harsh painful realty of Dad's death.

When things went bad, I fantasized. I would create unbelievable scenarios that made life more acceptable, or, in my case, less painful.

Eventually, however I would come to my senses and realize that Dad was gone forever. When I experienced the truth every once in a while, I would become angry at the world, and myself, vowing to strike out before I get hurt again.

It would be a long time before I was ready to trust others, and share the impact of this experience. It would take a miracle for me to ever reach a place when I could function in a healthy, constructive, and honest world. I immersed myself into a world dictated by anger, towards others and toward myself. Over the years I have asked myself so many questions about Dad's death. I have never allowed myself to share these questions with anyone. The impact of Dad's death would haunt me for the next three decades. I operated from a position where the residue from this trauma would affect my every action, my every thought, my every feeling. It would interfere with my ability to have lasting, meaningful relationships. It impacted how I viewed myself and how I viewed others. It affected my ability to trust. I had lost the ability to trust anyone, especially men in authority, and adults in general. I would experience feelings of inadequacy as a young man, and eventually as an adult. The image of death would forever be a source of horror in my world. The price I paid for allowing myself to get close to people was too high. Whenever I trusted another person, I got hurt. Whenever I felt love toward another human being, they would die. I walked through life believing that I was "jinxed". I thought that if anyone got too close to me, they would die. I felt I had the power to end other people's lives.

From the day I was told that Dad had died until I was approximately twelve years old, I do not remember very much. I know I still attended school, I was involved in sports, I had some friends, and I probably went on in life the best I could. But during this period in my life I have blocked out most of my memories. Basically everything up to this time in my life was a blur.

Entering my pre-teen years proved to be very painful. By this time my brother and I had developed reputations as two brothers to stay clear of. Most of my lasting relationships were based on lying, stealing, destroying property, defying authority, hurting others, and fighting. We would soon create a gang of friends that would stand by us through thick and thin.

We would soon start to carry knives, chains, and whatever we could use to protect ourselves and hurt others.

At a period of time in most young men's lives when they are undergoing a change from childhood into adolescence and establishing a way of life that would create a successful future, my brother and I were on a self-destructive journey. This way of living would have dire consequences for us, and for those we came into contact with. We were both walking time bombs. Where we exploded could never be determined. But we did it a little differently. Jeff exploded outward, while I exploded inward.

The Ultimate Escape (age 12)

As I entered adolescence I soon found a way to forget all the thoughts and emotions I was experiencing. I do not recall how this happened, but I remember I started to smoke cigarettes with my buds. Soon after I was introduced to inhalants such airplane glue, nail polish remover, and a cleaning solvent called "Medi-mist". The effect that inhaling these substances had on me was incredible, and a welcome relief to the anguish and pain that it replaced. The experience of being high, or in an altered state of consciousness was amazing. I could abandon all my inhibitions and produce a pleasant state of mind and body. I loved to get stoned on whatever I could find. It didn't matter what it was or how I had to take it. I was hooked from the first high.

Soon after using inhalants I started to drink alcohol. The first time I drank beer I "blacked out". I woke up the next afternoon with absolutely no memory of what had taken place after my fourth beer. This scared me quite a bit because I was the type of person who needed to know where I was and what I was doing. At all times I needed to be alert to my surroundings, so as not too become vulnerable or exposed to danger. But this tinge of fear was very quickly replaced by the need to get drunk again. I got right back into the beer that following early afternoon, resolving to have a better memory.

In a very short period of time I was introduced to a variety of drugs that I embellished.

I took them in different ways, but they all produced amazing results. Thus I learned to alter my reality through the use of many different types. This all started at age 12. In a short time I had used pot, hash, hash oil, MDA, mescaline, LSD, mushrooms, cocaine, and eventually speed. Each had different affects yet they all served the same purpose. They took me away from that dark place and helped me feel something other than pain. These chemicals made me feel bigger than life. They helped me to laugh and have fun; I didn't feel as uncomfortable around other people; they introduced me to a whole lot of new friends; they helped me behave in ways that I usually wouldn't. They helped me to forget, even for a brief period of time, all the crap in my life.

So I dove into a world of alcohol and drug abuse. Addiction would eventually take a firm grasp on every aspect of my life, and almost end my life on dozens of different occasions.

Little did I know at the time that I was creating a "monster" inside. Or was it possible that the monster already existed? I did not know that all the pain and anguish I had already experienced in life would be nothing compared to results of abusing substances. Whatever came first, the addict or the monster, it really doesn't matter. I do know that from the first time I got "high" to the last time I used anything, I created a personal hell that would affect all areas of my life, and one that would nearly cost me my life. This personal hell was far worse than anything I had experienced.

I experienced very early in my substance use that there was a price to pay for escaping reality.

Often I would lose track of time, places, and events. I was more susceptible to violent outbursts of uncontrollable rage. Any one close to me could be hurt by my episodes, but in a majority of situations I would take it out on myself. On a regular basis I would wake up in the hospital being treated for self-inflicted injuries or injuries that were the result of an outburst. I soon realized that if I got too "out of it" I had absolutely no control of the outcome. Nine out of ten times I was prepared to take this risk only to find myself in the hospital, or recalling how I almost got killed the evening before.

As much as I wanted to escape from pain, all I did was create more.

My early teens were spent wandering from one drug to another, from party to another and from one disaster to another. Our basement was dubbed, "The Ultimate Den of Iniquity" by my own mother. As teens, my brother and I were the identified as the leaders of a gang. We were two brothers you never crossed. We accepted these roles with pride and set out to ensure that everyone would know who we were.

Another problem I developed during these chemical fuelled years was I could not escape the inner pain and turmoil that I felt. As much as the drugs and alcohol helped me escape from my problems, I could never be totally sure when I would become violent, depressed, and suicidal. My pension for getting totally wasted was uncontrollable from the onset. From the age of 12 until 17, I lost so much time, respect and so many friendships that I do not care to count. The following is a history of my early to mid-teens.

At age 11 and a half I started sniffing glue, nail polish remover, and Medi-Mist. I would sniff to the point where I could not walk, talk, or even stand up.

At age 12 I blacked out the first time I drank alcohol.

At age 12 I was introduced to pot and hashish.

At ages 13, 14, and 15, I was hospitalized on eight separate occasions for various self-inflicted injuries and three overdoses. During one of these nights I attempted to break into a neighbor's home by putting my fist through a 3x6 windowpane. This resulted in 12 stitches in my left hand. Within a week of this incident I almost had to have my left thumb amputated due to a serious infection.

At age 13 I started to use MDA, mescaline, LSD, and cocaine frequently.

At age 15 I was charged with being under age in a drinking establishment, and Possession of an Offensive Weapon Dangerous to the Public Peace. During this same year I was nearly run over by a train.

At age 15 I also started shooting speed. I injected it several times a day for about two weeks consecutively. By the last day I knew that if I didn't stop I would die.

Later this year I ate so much LSD that I was hospitalized. I remained stoned for nearly three days.

By age 15 the only real comfort I had from all this craziness was my first true girlfriend. Cathy and I met at a summer job and I fell in love with her. She was everything I needed in a girlfriend and she was incredibly patient and supportive with me as I continued to struggled. But by now I have quit school entirely, managing to complete half of grade 10.

Throughout all these years there were thousands of episodes of blackout drinking, and numerous acts of violence toward others and myself.

So it's Sunday morning around 5:30am. I am now 14 years old and I was just released from the Wellesley Hospital in downtown Toronto. I am seriously contemplating suicide. It just turns out that the Glen Road Bridge is on the way home. It is the only way I know that all this pain and bullshit will go away. I have no other option at this point in my life. I am a complete failure. I suck at everything. I hate school and sports. I don't have any real friends. I cannot control my actions, my thoughts, my feelings. I get extremely violent so quickly that it even scares the crap out of me. I want to hurt others and myself. I hate this world and I hate myself. I'm a skinny little bastard who feels worthless. Nothing in my life makes any sense to me. This world sucks, my life sucks, I hate everything, and everything hates me. Luck may have it that I didn't jump off the bridge but went home and fell asleep before anyone was up. (Great, more nightmares, more violence – when's it all going to stop?)

L S D

I was introduced to LSD in grade 7. I initially felt scared of the hallucinations and images that I experienced, but like every drug I tried I grew to love it. At first there were different types of blotters, orange, red, purple microdot and so on. It seemed almost crazy to me that you could get so out of it by eating a piece of paper with a dot on it. I never really understood how this drug worked yet I continued to eat it at an alarming rate. I soon found out that there were many other types of acid, and some that were very, very powerful. One was called Three-Eyed-Toad. Yeah, it was a piece of paper with a picture of a toad that had three eyes; pretty freakin' weird. But man could you get blasted on this. Another form of acid that really screwed me up was Window Pane. In the course of several years I consumed LSD roughly 60 times. Each trip was just as good as the one previous, yet there were times I thought I was going to lose my mind. And I hated coming down from this drug. It took forever, and the coming down was a several hour period that was full of guilt, shame, remorse, and depression. Life would eventually return to the way it was meant to be. But I was fully conscious of how much life depressed me. I experienced countless thoughts of ending my life during these times. I wanted so desperately to sleep but could not. I wanted to shut my brain down but it was full of self-harming plans and periods of extreme and pain. I vowed each time to stop taking acid yet each time it became available I gobbled it up with a fury. The need for me to laugh and get wasted was far greater than the consequences of my actions. I could never seem to stop and ask myself, "Is this really worth it?"

It was Friday evening, and I was scheduled for an interview at a boy's private school at 9:00am Saturday. It was a two-hour drive to the school. It was nearing the end of grade eight and I just recently had a major meeting with the administration of my Sr. Public School. The school indicated that they were unable to refer me to any High School in Toronto due to my performance, attendance and my overall grades. I was screwed.

I really had no option but to attend a Trade School where there was plenty of violence, drugs, and pain. I refused to accept a referral to any such school.

My mom located a Boys Private School in Newmarket, Ontario, that professed to work wonders with students just like me. My options boiled down to Trade or Private School. I chose to attend an interview with my mother in Newmarket, in the hope of beginning my grade nine academic school year off to a fresh start.

My mom called the Headmaster of this school and scheduled an interview for 9:00am Saturday morning.

So it's Friday evening. I have this plan in my head that I'm going up to Northern Secondary, score something to get high on, enjoy the band in the gym, and return home. Just as I'm getting ready to head out my mom approaches me and asks where I'm going.

"I'm heading up to catch a band at Northern Secondary."

"David, I really think you should stay home tonight and get some rest. Remember we have a 9:00am appointment with the Head Master tomorrow."

"Yeah I remember, but I don't feel like sitting around all evening."

"Well I'm worried that you might be out later than you planned and not be rested for this meeting. It's really important that you're rested for this interview. This is your future we are planning for."

"Well I'm not going to sit around here all night."

"Well I think it would be best…"

"Ahh fuck off – you always think you know what's best for me, I wish you would just leave me the fuck alone."

I pushed my way past her and slammed the door on the way out.

I was pissed off as I walked down the street to catch the bus. My head was full of resentful, mean thoughts. My pulse was rapid and I was hyperventilating. My heart was pounding, I felt like it could explode at any moment. I felt as though I could kill the next person who got in my way. I was angry, scared, and remorseful all at the same time. I wanted to hurt someone, not necessarily my mom but someone, anyone. But as usual I always ended up turning my anger toward myself. I knew that something shitty was going to happen but I didn't give a crap. I'll take anything on – anything!

Why does Mom always think she knows what best for me? I'll do whatever I want to and there is no one in this whole fucking world that can stop me. I would welcome anyone to try and stop me. I would love nothing better than to mess someone up.

By the time I took the bus to the subway, transferred to the train, and connected with another bus that took me to the High School I was ready to take on the world. I searched frantically for John who always had something to eat or smoke. He was a real freak. He had long black curly hair, a beard that hadn't been trimmed for weeks, always in jeans and a jean-jacket, and always ready to turn you on. I finally found John in the men's bathroom.

"Hey John, do you got anything?"

"Hey Dave, all I got is acid."

"How much?"

"Five bucks for two hits."

"I'll take two then."

Imagine, five bucks and I was able to get wasted. Not just for a little while but all night.

I could not wait to get relief inside my head. It was the only relief I had from all the bullshit in this world.

John met me at the sink counter. He reached into his jean jacket and pulled out a plastic sandwich bag. He rolled it open and out dropped several aluminum foils all rolled up. He took one, opened it and showed me two tiny clear pieces of plastic. I couldn't believe what I was seeing. I had never seen this type of acid before, and it almost looked fake. But John would never rip me off. He knows I would likely beat the crap out of him if he did. He had never ripped me off before. Maybe this would be the first time. I was about to ask him about this acid when he stared at me straight in the eyes and said,

"David, you will only need one quarter of one of these. Cut both these into four quarters. Only eat one quarter, and no more."

He resembled a doctor prescribing medication to his patient. He informed me how much I was to take. He was very clear about his instructions, and appeared very serious too. Of course John didn't really didn't know who he was talking to. I know what I'm doing. I had scored drugs from him so many times that I should be the one prescribing to him just how much I could handle.

Of course I knew that he was full of shit, as I has done so much acid that there was no way one little quarter of this windowpane would be enough. He must have thought he was really clever telling me how much LSD I could handle. But being an attentive little doper I followed his instructions to a tee. I opened my little foil and laid out on the bathroom counter two tiny, clear slabs of acid approximately ¼ of an inch by ¼ of an inch. I methodically cut the little plastic sheets into four quarters, leaving me with a total of eight cut pieces. I licked the tip of my index finger and lifted one quarter from the counter to my mouth. I then folded the remaining seven quarters into the foil and headed out into the gym. I remember feeling extremely anxious and impatient. I wanted to get high and the sooner the better. I was also excited as I watched the band set up their equipment. I always felt a particular rush being around bands and their equipment. I wished that I could own all the gear that they had. I watched intently as they positioned their equipment into place, tuning their instruments, setting the microphones up, and so on. I started to realize that I was not feeling any effects of the acid I had eaten about a half an hour earlier. I decided to return to the bathroom to eat some more. As I moistened my finger again and lifted another quarter to my mouth I paused for a brief second as I heard John's voice say to me:

"David, you will only need one quarter of these, only eat one quarter and no more."

I placed the second quarter into my mouth and headed back out to the gym. Within a half hour I was back in the bathroom eating two more quarters for a total of one whole tab of acid. Within another 40 minutes I returned to the bathroom and ate the remaining four quarters. This brought to a total of 8 quarters (or two whole tabs) of windowpane acid that I ate within an hour and a half of arriving at the school. The last thing I vaguely remember was standing in the gymnasium watching the band getting ready to play. I do not remember much from this point in the evening until about 4:00am. One of my best friends, Ian, was looking all over the school for me. He knew I had rough night with my mom. He also knew I had a bunch of acid, and he was worried. He finally located me in the back of the school riding a 10-speed bike around the track. He knew I was in trouble.

He ran out to the track and grabbed the handlebars of this bike, which brought me to a complete stop. I vaguely remember him stepping in front of the bike and grabbing the handlebars. I remember seeing his skeleton hands and knuckles grasping the handlebars. I could faintly hear him asking me something. I looked up from my position and I saw my friend as he struggled to speak to me. His face was different though; his facial features were all distorted and moving around. I could barely see any resemblance to my buddy, yet I knew it was him. When he spoke he sounded with a 45 being played at 33rpms. I barely made out what he said.

Ian said, *"Arrrrrre yyyoouuuu ooooookkkkkay?"*

His words echoed in my brain I looked up from the handlebars and stared Ian right in the face. But it didn't look like Ian. His entire face was shifting and swaying back and forth. I could see his mouth moving but I couldn't make out what he was saying. I tried desperately to answer him but I could not speak. I briefly glanced over his shoulder and watched as the trees in the rear of the school, about six of them, all resembled Medusa's Hair, with snakes wiggling out of them all. I looked back to Ian and shook my head indicating, "NO, I'M NOT OK!"

I'm guessing that at this point in the evening it's roughly 9:30pm. The next thing I remember was regaining consciousness and sitting across the table from this older woman. I was still hallucinating from the acid but at least I could talk now. I asked her,

"Where am I?"

"You are at Cathy's home, I am her mother."

"How did I get here?"

"I came to pick you up at Northern Secondary around 9:30."

"What time is it now?"

"It's almost four in the morning."

I sat with this kind woman for another hour or so. She went on to explain that I was experiencing a very bad acid trip when my buddy Ian phoned her daughter Cathy. Cathy called her to ask for help. Cathy's mom, a registered nurse, drove over to the school to pick me up. After arriving at her home around 10pm, she persuaded me to take six Valium and gave me roughly a half dozen beer to counteract the chemical in my system. We basically sat at her kitchen table for several hours as she talked me down from the bad trip I was on. None of this I remember. The last thing I recall was being in the washroom at the school. I do not remember anything until I came to at her kitchen table. I was still peaking on the acid and the entire kitchen appeared to be pulsating, almost breathing, in and out, the walls swaying back and forth.

But as I sat with this woman I knew that I was going to be ok. I wanted so badly to be straight. I wanted so badly not to be tripping on this acid. I wanted so badly to feel normal. After some more talk Cathy's mom asked if I felt I could go home now. I nodded yes.

This kind, patient lady offered to drive me home. I sat mostly in silence all the way to my home. I recall coming to a stop across the street from our home. I tried my best to thank her for saving my life. I'm sure my words were slurred and inaudible.

I got out of the car and walked across the street to my house. I walked up the steps to the front veranda. I opened the screen door and found the main door locked. I knocked quietly, not wanting to disturb anyone, yet not wanting to spend the rest of the night on the front steps. I could hear my mom coming down the stairs and unlocking the front door. I stood at the door with my head hung down, ashamed to look her in the eyes. The conversation we had when I left the house earlier that evening echoed in my brain. I cannot believe I swore at her. I cannot understand why I would treat my mom this way. I hated myself. I wanted to die right on the front steps of my home. Maybe it would better if I were dead. Maybe the world would be a better place without someone like me. The hatred I had toward myself was unbearable.

She opened the door and in her compassionate way asked if I was ok.

"No Mom, I took a lot of LSD tonight and I had a really bad experience." Still looking down.

"Do you think you will be able to sleep?"

"No Mom, but I will try, Mom . . . . I'm really sorry for being so rude to you."

This was not the first time I had used acid, but it was my last.

I must have passed out in my bed because I woke up to hear my little sister's voice. She was shaking me and saying,

"David, David, you have to get up. You have an interview in a couple of hours."

I don't know how I got ready, cleaned up, dressed and into the car. But as soon as we started to drive I crashed out again. The next thing I remember is my mom trying to wake me up.

"David, David, you have to wake up. We are at the College, and you need to wake up."

I don't remember getting out of the car, or walking into the school. I remember falling asleep in the Headmaster's waiting room while my mom and he had a chat. I recall my mom waking me up and saying that I needed to participate in the interview. I sat across from the Headmaster with my mom at my side. I do not recall what was said in the interview. I remember him asking me questions and waiting for some kind of a response from me. He would ask me a question, and as he did his head would bob up and down. I almost started laughing out loud as I thought he looked like a turtle as he spoke. He sounded like one too. The harder I tried to communicate the worse it got. Finally my mom piped in and said,

"Mr. B., my son was out last night and took some drugs. He had a very bad experience and is not really able to communicate today."

"Yes, I see," nodded Mr. B. "David, could you please wait in the reception room and we will get back to you very soon?"

Guess what? I fell asleep in the Headmaster's waiting room again. The next thing I remember was my mom waking me up telling me that Mr. B. wanted to talk with me.

I went back into his office. He made it very clear, as only a turtle can, that if I was to attend the College that I could not be taking any drugs/alcohol. He also made it perfectly clear that I was welcome to attend the College in September.

My teen years were worse than my earlier years. The difference was that now I was on a self-destructive mode. I was out of control with my alcohol and drug use. The harder I tried to escape my reality, the worse my self-destructive nature got. The harder I tried to avoid my feelings, my thoughts, and my behavior, the more all of these things intensified. No matter what drug or drink I took, I would always return to the place inside me that said I was NO GOOD! It seemed as though I was destined to live a life that was dictated by my strong hatred for myself. The harder I fought against myself, the more I lost. I was in a Catch 22; the harder I tried, the worse things got. It would take nothing short of a miracle to change the way I operated in this world.

You see, once a guy like me experiences a bit of freedom, it is really difficult to accept controls, restrictions, and rules. The potential for disaster to occur was extremely high.

To do a complete 360 degree change without a life-changing experience was next to impossible. I could not say no to my friends or tell them that I wanted to turn over a new leaf. I wanted desperately to say these words but my precious ego would not allow it. I wanted to stop drinking and drugging yet the pressure to use was always all around me. I wanted to be successful at something in life but I did not know how to succeed.

I wanted to stop abusing myself, but I hated myself too much. I wanted to not hurt others yet I made a promise when I was eight that was still ingrained in my soul.

I have met so many other young people who operate this way. They are so entrenched in their anger at the world that they will not let their inner potential emerge. Well I'm here to say that it doesn't have to be this way. If I can find meaning in my crazy little world, then so can anybody. If I can find one thing in life that is important to me than anyone can. If I can change from an angry, violent, self-destructive youth into a caring, healthy adult, then anyone can.

But it would take the near impossible to happen in order for any long-lasting change to occur.

It is my belief that everyone has a purpose in this life. There is a place for everyone to be productive, contributing human beings. Some of us are takers, while others are givers. Having been a taker all my life, I would need to find that something special for me. But how does an angry young man find purpose in his life? Where does he go and who does he talk to in order to understand his purpose in life?

How does this transformation begin, and what are the steps a person like me can take to get well. I truly believed that if some sort of miracle didn't happen soon that I was destined to become another teenage statistic. Yeah. Another young Aboriginal male who gave up. Another teenager wastes all his potential. Just one more youth who lost the battle to stay alive.

Everyone Has A Special Gift

It was during my early teens that I developed an interest in music. I remember returning home late one night after an evening of partying, and I was stumbling around in the basement. I went upstairs and found myself in our dining room where my dad's guitar and upright piano were positioned. I was flooded with thoughts of dad as I opened his guitar case and reached for his guitar. All I could do was hold it, hugging it, rocking back and forth and sobbing for the little boy I used to be. I felt as though I would never stop crying as there was so much pain buried deep in my soul. I decided that I needed rest so I tucked his guitar back in its bed and me into mine.

As time passed I taught myself to play dad's guitar by mimicking the finger positions he used, just as I remembered them. I didn't realize how much I focused on his skills as he played. How I must have examined his every move. I started to teach myself how to handle this instrument, just as he had.

It was also during my early teens I found myself drawn toward the neighborhood children. Yeah, me. The guy who can't do anything right, who is always out of it, and who really doesn't care whether he lived or died. I experienced a special bond with the kids who lived on our street. I cherished their unconditional acceptance of me and was able to return affection to them by being available to them for fun, games, street hockey, field trips etc. I spent literally hundreds of hours playing with these children and it seemed the more I gave, the more I got in return. I knew every child on the block as well as their families. Each spare minute was spent with Sandi, David, Michael, Crocky, Ian, Rod, Joel, John, my little brother Sean, and so on and so on. There were so many special younger children on our street I can't begin to name each one of them. We would spend so many hours playing, laughing, and having fun that there were times I didn't want the fun to stop. There were so many kids in our neighborhood and each one of them has a special place in my heart. I will never forget how their friendship impacted me. I learned to feel love for others and yes I loved each of my friends. They will never know how they helped to change my life. They will never know how much I loved them all. They made me feel important and accepted. No one had done this before and I will never forget any of them – Never!

But I refused to let them see my self-destructive side. What they needed was more important to me than what I needed. What they needed in an older male role model and friend was more important to me than my own selfish needs. They started to teach me the meaning of giving unconditionally. These children brought out the best in me. They accepted me for the kind, humorous person I could be, and they helped shape the young man I wanted to be. The unfortunate part was I had created a Dr. Jekyll & Mr. Hyde complex. When I was good, I was really good; but when I was bad, watch out.

I would soon come to realize that I would always have to control which person I would be. I could only do this when I was straight however. Sooner or later these two personalities would collide. One day one personality would have to conquer the other. Then this battle of battles would erupt, and it would almost cost me my life. I didn't know that then, but I would find out soon enough.

My passion for playing with the neighborhood children did not go unnoticed. As I continued to struggle personally, academically, and socially I was able to somehow complete grade 9, with the assistance of a structured learning environment at a boy's private school in southern Ontario. It was at this institution that I was able to perform at an above average level and, for the first time since I could remember, experience academic success. I demonstrated that I had the ability to learn in a school setting, and produced positive results in the area of athletics as well.

But accepting success did not come easily to me. The experience of success became a threat to what I had been so accustomed to, that of being a failure. So the more success I experienced the more I set out to sabotage all the progress I had made. I attribute this underlying "failure to thrive" disorder as concrete evidence that the internal battle within my soul, the good guy vs. the bad guy, would surface and I would eventually return to my comfort zone of failure. It is amazing that in my world, to succeed meant that there might be something positive inside me, which could override any negative self-doubt. This constant inner conflict would continue to surface. I somehow knew I had the potential to succeed, and even desired this to a great extent; yet my inner most being dictated that I would eventually return to the pain, despair and anger, which would convince me to act out, become violent, and lose everything I wanted so much in life.

In any event, I left the only academic setting where I could produce positive results and returned to Toronto to register at a local high school. I left the safety and support of a private school to return to the scene in the big city. It wasn't long before I was immersed in the alcohol, drug, and violent sub-cultures.

My experience at this high school only reinforced the negative outlook I had on myself. I was fifteen years old when the administration at the High School arranged a meeting with my mom and myself. As I sat there in the presence of one principal, two vice–principals, a school counselor, my homeroom teacher, and my mom, I felt terribly out-numbered. It was the entire school administration against me. It took every ounce of courage I could find in me to not get up, tell everyone where to go, and slam the door on the way out. Believe me, I thought about it several times during that brief meeting. You see, the school staff already had an agenda. This is what they told me:

"David, even if you applied yourself 110% for the remaining half of this academic year, even if you did all your homework every night, and did some extra work to cover what I had already missed, YOU WOULD NOT SUCCESSFULLY COMPLETE THE SCHOOL YEAR!"

This meeting took place in December, and armed with this information I stood up, told everyone there to fuck off, left the office, and slammed the door behind me. Immediately I set out to continue my destructive life-style, with a renewed conviction. Within a year and a half I been expelled from three high schools in Toronto. At the ripe age of 16, I was a high school dropout, with no direction in life.

It was my last day at my fourth High School in Toronto. Another year in grade ten ruined. It was a fall afternoon and our school was hosting a football game. As usual most of the students were in the bleachers cheering for the home school while my close buddies, my brother, and I were consuming drinks and drugs under the bleachers. We were invincible. No one in their right mind would interfere with our little get together. Now I'm almost positive that other students partied during these events, but for some reason or another they never seemed to get into trouble. They seemed to be able to handle themselves at functions like this. They probably had a few drinks, cheered for their favorite team, and went home for dinner. We always seemed to attract trouble, and at times went looking for it. This occasion we went looking for it.

Following half time break we collectively decided to enter the school and lay a beating on one of the school administrators. The school office sent out an emergency message over the school PA requesting immediate assistance from all male teachers on site. What resulted was a gang style battle between our boys and several school staff, including two Phys Ed teachers. I had already blacked out from the drugs and alcohol, and the last thing I remember was watching my buddy Steven jump on the back of one of the Phys Ed Teachers and start to pounding the side of his face repeatedly. Of course I was expelled from the school and we were all given lifetime bans from being on school property. Not to mention several charges which were eventually dismissed. To this day I have never set foot near this school again. It was also during my brief stay at this school when I spent a great deal of time on my own. I did not make friends easily and ones I already knew were drinkers and druggies. When most students ate their lunches in the school cafeteria during lunch break, you would often find me at the lounge across the street enjoying several beers. I learned later in my life that these were often referred to as "liquid lunches". I was fifteen, expelled from my fourth High School, and going nowhere.

It was during this particular summer I was employed at a summer camp near Haliburton, Ontario. I had a couple days off and my brother showed up at the camp. He invited me into the small town of Minden to go for a few draughts. An offer I could not refuse. We hitchhiked into Minden and entered the men's only side of the bar. The other side was restricted for women and their escorts. We ordered several twenty-five cent draughts and sat down. As we were sitting there I started to feel a bit uncomfortable, but I did not know why. My brother and I chatted for a few minutes before another resident of this small community entered the bar. I do not remember his name but my brother and I both knew him. He joined us at the table and immediately started to joke with me.

He said, *"Hey, I'll bet you a draught that I can make you say the same color twice."*

I responded by saying, *"Fuck off, there's no way you can make me do anything."*

He continued, *"Well pick a color, any color."*

"Blue."

"What did you say?"

"I said blue."

Well the little shit. He did it. He made me repeat the color I had chosen. We broke out laughing and I thought this was great. I told him to help himself to a beer and I stood up and decided that I was going to try this on someone else.

I approached another table, and as soon I made eye contact with one of the patrons, I called out to him,

"Hey buddy, I'll bet you a draught I can make you say the same color twice."

"You're on."

"Pick a color, any color."

"Red."

"Beg your pardon?

"RED, oh shit!"

We both broke out laughing as he offered me a glass of beer. I declined the beer and said I had to try this again.

I walked toward another table were six guys were seated.

"Hey buddy, I'll bet you a draught I can make you say the same color twice."

"FUCK OFF!"

I stopped, almost frozen, then decided to walk away from this table. As I took a few steps away he repeated:

"Fuck off, you dirty Indian."

My blood started boiling. My temperature rose significantly. My ears started to throb. I could feel my heartbeat pound from my ears. I stopped again, turned around, and walked a few steps back to their table.

"Who said that?"

Five guys pointed to one fella seated closest to where I stood.

"What the fuck's your problem?"

He stood up, stepped toward me and we stood eye-to-eye. It was then that I realized he must be at least six feet tall. As we stood face-to-face, or should I say face-to-chest, I decided that I wasn't backing down. No fucking idiot was going to call me a dirty Indian and walk away.

"What the fuck is your problem?" I repeated.

"Hey we don't like Indians coming in here and bumming beer!"

"Listen asshole, it was a fucking joke. I don't want your god damn beer. I can pay for my own. Or are you so retarded that you don't know a joke when you hear one?"

"Listen here Indian…"

"Shut your fucking mouth or I'll shut it for you!"

"So you want to take this outside, Indian?"

"Right fuckin' now asshole."

We walked to the side of the bar and exited through a door that lead outside. We were standing there face-to-chest and I tried to tell him once again that I was joking, and I didn't want his beer. I watched him look down at the sheath that was attached to my belt. He looked me in the eyes and said,

"So, I see you have a knife. Do you plan to use it?"

"If I have to I will."

He took three steps to the door we just exited, whistled, and another six or so men ran out to surround me. I remember thinking to myself, *"I'M GOING TO DIE!"*

I was standing toe-to-toe with this six-foot cowboy and surrounded by twelve of his buddies. (I did a quick count once they were all out of the bar).

And then I thought, *"WHERE THE FUCK IS MY BROTHER?"*

At that moment by brother burst through the ring of idiots that had surrounded me. Now we both stood toe-to-toe with this big brute.

"What the fuck is in going on?"

"Your brother is bumming beer in our tavern."

"I was telling you a fucking joke."

"I guess you have a knife too?"

My brother pulls out of his jacket pocket a six inch switch-blade, triggers it open, waves it in front of this goon's face, retracts the blade and places it back in his pocket.

"Are you going to use it?"

"Only if I have to."

Within a split second our knives are out and we are swinging and slashing anyone who came within arm's reach. During this chaos I notice that one guy had my brother down and was pounding on his face near the curb to the road. I managed to run to him and kick the fella on top right in the ribs with all my strength. The impact of my foot connecting with his ribs made a crunching sound that I can still hear to this day. I watched as he fell off my brother and collapsed on the road. I do not remember if he ever got up again. The punching, kicking, slashing continued for what seemed an hour. More realistically it was about fifteen minutes when the OPP, with their lights flashing, screeched to a halt on the main road in Minden, drew their guns, and yelled for everyone to stand still. One officer approached the first goon I met in the tavern and asked what happened. He told the officer that the two of us were in the tavern, bumming beer, and waving knives around.

They immediately handcuffed my brother and I and virtually threw us into the back of their vehicle. The same officer then turned to a crowd of a dozen or so men and asked if a couple of volunteers would come to the station to fill out a statement.

As we pulled away from the tavern I looked back to see that several men were holding wounds to their arms and upper bodies, and the guy I kicked was still lying on the curb with two others bending over him.

We spent Saturday in the Minden jail. On Sunday we drove 120 miles per hour to the nearest town with a court building where we spent Sunday night. We were brought before a Judge Monday morning. We were released on our own recognizance and we returned to Haliburton. Word quickly got out about this event. I was sure that it would cost me my job at the camp. Apparently the camp staff held a meeting and unanimously voted to have me return to work.

It took approximately twelve months to answer to the charges of

a.   Being under age in a licensed establishment.
b.   Possession of an Offensive Weapon Dangerous To the Public Peace.
c.   Assault with a Deadly Weapon.
d.   Assault causing Bodily Harm.

Our day in court was June of the following year. Evidence was brought forward that all, or most of the fellas we fought were in their late twenties and early thirties, and that the two men who had sworn statements against us were in jail on assault charges. After the summer I returned to Toronto and had a dismal time trying to find a job. Like who the hell is going to hire a grade 9 drop out with no skills or training? I got work in a warehouse in downtown TO. This lasted for a couple of paychecks, after which I screwed off. I was sixteen, unemployed, had a criminal record, and still going nowhere fast.

But I was still able to keep up with all the kids in the neighborhood. This was my only source of comfort. This was the only area in my life that I felt good about.

I sought out and located a College Preparation Program at Seneca College in Toronto. I registered for in this program in the fall of 1972. I was seventeen years old.

It was in this program where discovered that I could not conceal my interest in working with people who were less off than myself. My class-mates and instructors all encouraged me to pursue a career on the helping profession. Of course I shrugged it off. It was easier for me to minimize my positive qualities, as I was still unable to accept positive feedback from others. Nonetheless, I completed this course with above average grades and more importantly, a sense of direction in my life.

It was one month before my 18th birthday in May 1973 that another person, John, approached me with an offer to work with emotionally dis-turbed children. This came as a complete shock to me as I felt I still had little to offer. But it took me less than a week to accept his offer, and set out to my new job as a Child Care Worker in Ontario.

I was seventeen years of age, and off on an adventure that would even-tually save my life. I am forever grateful to John for taking a chance on me. He saw something in me that I could never have seen on my own. Someday I would like to locate this man and let him know what he did for me.

He provided me with a way out of my dismal existence. He started my training to become a professional, caring, human being. He reached out to me at the most crucial time in my life. I did not know what I was getting myself into, yet I knew it had to be better than what I was doing.

On Monday May 24, 1973 I reported to a group home for my first day at work as a Child Care Worker at the ripe old age of seventeen, and scared shitless. I was sure that they would likely send me home before the end of the day after they realized what a huge mistake they had made. They did not know me, nor I them. They seemed like nice enough people yet they had no idea what kind of person I had become. They had no idea of the type of violence I was capable of. They didn't know how I was capable of flying off the handle. They couldn't have known the many different types of drugs/booze I had been involved in all these years. All they knew was my reputation in Toronto with all the kids in the neighborhood. They were willing and ready to give me an opportunity based on the opinion of one person, John B.

You see, one of my little friends on our street was sent to a group home in Barrie, Ontario. I was really worried about where he had gone so I requested from his mother that I be able to visit him. He was sent to a group home for emotionally disturbed children and I had to make arrangements to visit him on the weekend. Imagine, a young thug from TO taking time on his weekend to visit a child from the neighborhood. This was another example of the good guy-bad guy dilemma I was experiencing.

I went to track down my little buddy, David. David lived on our street in Rosedale. His family lived two doors down the street from me. He was so special to me and I grew to love this little guy so much. Wow! It's amazing, but I was able to reach out and love another person! I was introduced to the profession of Child Care Work. I was really impressed with the quality of care that my little friend received. I had never known that it was possible to have a job, let alone a career working with children. So I decided to take John up on his offer and accepted work at a one of their group homes in, of all places, Haliburton, Ontario. It was at this group home where I was first taught to develop my skills as a professional helper. I worked alongside many caring co-workers who provided me with direction and support. They taught me how to make a positive connection with a young person who was been hurt through negligence and abuse. I learned how to help children reach into their pain and fear. I comforted them as they cried out in pain and anger. I reassured them as they struggled to make sense out of their personal trauma. And I laughed and played with them as I had done for so long with the kids on Standish

Avenue in Toronto. That was the fun part of my work. I didn't need any direction when it came to playing and having fun with these children. I was gifted at this part of the work. It came naturally for me to play, joke around, and laugh with these children. I was very capable of being a child myself. I did not hesitate to get really involved in their play. I had an amazing imagination for play. I had a gift for this type of interaction with these children.

I remained employed with this organization for nearly three years. Each year taught me more and more about the methods required to treat young people who suffered from family violence experiences and the emotional impact of this abuse. I resigned from this job in March 1976 and set out to seek my fame and fortune in the Western Provinces of Canada. I decided to leave Ontario, my family, my friends, the drugs, the booze and travel to Vancouver, BC. A quick trip by train and I landed in Edmonton, Alberta. It was April, 1976. I didn't know a single person in this city. I was virtually on my own without any supports. I checked into a downtown hotel, and within two weeks I landed a full time job as an Adolescent Therapy Counsellor with the Alberta Government. Again I surrounded myself with caring and loving supports through my work. My trip to Alberta would prove to be the best decision I had made to this point in my life. My girlfriend moved to Alberta with me in April, 1976, we were married in 1977, and divorced in 1979. This would eventually be the first of three marriages that I would have. This first one was full of work, drinking, drugging, and fighting. It was the worst relationship I had ever been in.

At this point in my journey, it is important to state that I had not taken any steps toward addressing the experiences from my childhood. I had not spoken to a single person about those years. My past was about to catch up with me in what would become a life/death confrontation. The time was fast approaching for me to either get help, or die. I worked extremely effectively with other children, youth, and families, but I had not yet stopped to look at myself. I still felt angry, scared, fearful, lost, lonely, and extremely sad inside.

I had not taken any time to try and fix what was really wrong with me. I wanted to live, but acted like I was ready to die.

What Happened

Every Addict Has Their Bottom

Following a two-year stint at my government job I hit rock bottom. In July, 1978, I left my job and home to live on the streets of downtown Edmonton. For ten days I drank, snorted drugs, smoked and ate anything I could get my hands on. Every waking moment went toward getting fucked up. I was bent on self-destruction, and nothing was going to get in my way. I became a walking, talking, ticking time bomb. I partied with whomever I could find, and slept wherever I could find a couch or a bed. I did not care about anything except getting high and drunk. I drank for ten days straight. I smoked drugs for ten days straight. I snorted drugs for ten days straight. I ate acid, MDA (ecstasy), and mushrooms. Whatever I could find, I did it.

I regained consciousness on the 11th day and for the first time in my 23 years on this planet I realized that if I continued to treat myself this way that I really would die. I was out of control. I could not stop myself from using drugs and/or alcohol. I was deathly afraid to leave my friend's town-house as I did not know where to go. I knew I would end up downtown getting wasted.

I phoned a professional friend who I had briefly spoken to before I left my position with the government. I went to see her and she made immediately arrangements for me to enter a detox centre in downtown Edmonton. I was 23 years old, and at the end of my rope. It was in detox that I learned that I suffered from a self-inflicted disease called alcoholism and drug addiction. I had hit bottom and I knew I needed help to understand why I behaved the way I did. Did anyone else behave and think the way I did? Did anyone else want to die like I did? Did anyone else hate himself or herself the way I hated myself? Was there anyone who struggled with this good guy vs. bad guy the way I did? Did anyone else drink to forget the pain, only to create more? Did anyone else hate the world the way I did? Was there anyone who could totally understand what it was like for me to be in my skin? Could anyone stop the merry-go-round in my brain? Could anyone at least slow the merry-go-round down a little, just so I could get some rest? It was in detox that I found what I had been searching for all this time.

A Place To Belong

I waited in the reception room for what seemed an eternity. I sat there shaking, sweating, and smelly. I hadn't bathed in a week. My mind raced a million miles a minute. I wanted to leave but had nowhere to go, I wanted to die but was afraid of death, I wanted to get high but I was scared I would overdose. I wanted to be loved but hated everyone. I wanted to sleep yet my nightmares were worse than anything I could ever imagine while awake. I wanted to live, but I didn't know what for. As I sat in the reception area I was sick, sweaty, smelly, and shaky. I struggled not to get up and walk out the door, back to the streets. As I sat there I noticed a pamphlet that was laying on the coffee table in front of me. For some unknown reason it caught my attention and I reached for it. I attempted to read the information on this pamphlet but I could not hold it still long enough. But I was curious about this little pamphlet. My curiosity was overwhelming. I had to know what it said. I picked it up and tried desperately to follow the instructions on the top of it. I vaguely recall is said something like: Ask yourself the following questions and answer them as honestly as you can. Honestly, well I could do this. It's not like it's a test or something. I walked over to the receptionist and requested a pen. She obliged. I returned to my seat and set out to be as honest as I could.

Are You An Alcoholic?

1. Do you lose time from work due to your drinking?
2. Is drinking making your home life unhappy?
3. Do you drink because you are shy with other people?
4. Is drinking affecting your reputation?
5. Have you ever felt remorse after drinking?
6. Have you gotten into financial difficulties as a result of drinking?
7. Do you turn to lower companions and an inferior environment when drinking?
8. Does you drinking make you careless of your family's welfare?
9. Has your ambition decreased since drinking?
10. Do you crave a drink at a definite time daily?
11. Do you want to drink the next morning?
12. Does drinking cause you difficulty in sleeping?
13. Has your efficiency decreased since drinking?
14. Is drinking jeopardizing your job or business?
15. Do you drink to escape from worries or trouble?
16. Do you drink alone?
17. Have you ever had a complete loss of memory as a result of drinking?
18. Has your physician ever treated you for drinking?
19. Do you drink to build up your self-confidence?
20. Have you ever been to a hospital or institution on account of drinking?

I answered yes to every question. I felt so proud of myself for being so honest. This is probably the first time in my 23 years that I passed with flying colors; I never scored 100% on anything.

And to think I could still be honest. I was so proud of myself. Just as I was celebrating the results of my effort when I noticed some fine print at the bottom of the page.

> If you have answered **YES** to any one of these questions,
> there is a definite warning that you may be alcoholic.

If you have answered **YES** to any two, the chances are you are an alcoholic.

If you have answered **YES** to three or more, you are definitely an alcoholic.

* (These Test Questions are used by John Hopkins University Hospital, Baltimore, MD, in deciding whether or not a patient is alcoholic.)

Well I immediately reacted to these comments. They tricked me, I thought. That's not fair. They should have told me before I checked off all these answers. What a sneaky way to trick someone into believing they are alcoholic.

Just as quickly however reality slapped me in the face.

"*I must be an alcoholic and a drug addict.*"

I certainly met the requirements and I was definitely at a loss as to what to do about it. Yeah, this is where I belonged. I decided then and there that I was going to find out as much as I could about this disease and that I would not leave this center until I was ready to. I was assigned to an Addictions Counselor named Vern. I grew quite attached to him, as he was the first person I had ever talked to about my alcohol and drug use. He also had long "hippie" type hair and looked as he had smoked a joint before he came to work. He also reminded me of John who sold me the Window Pane Acid in High School. I stayed with the program, even tried to participate as much as I could and exactly seventeen days later I accepted a certificate indicating that I had completed the program. I was asked to say a few words as I received this prestigious honor, and I slowly made my way to the front of the group, and stood at the podium.

"*Mmmmy nnnnname is David aaaandd I I I I I I I'm aaannnn alcoholic.*"

I was shaking with nerves. I had never said these words before to anyone, let alone a room full of recovering alcoholics, their families, and all the staff of the Detox Centre. I don't recall what pearls of wisdom I shared but I felt incredibly proud of myself for this miraculous step into the world of recovery. This was the first certificate I had ever received that proved that I had completed something. I had not taken any alcohol or drugs for 17 days.

But I knew that the next step I would take would require hard work. So after Detox I scheduled an appointment with my Social Worker friend who had initially referred me to Detox. She recommended that I continue my treatment in a therapeutic hospital program. My next move was to voluntarily admit myself into a Psychiatric Day Program at one of the local hospitals. I knew that my participation in this program would require that I attend eight hours a day, five days a week, for roughly six months. The intake worker also stated that I needed to remain alcohol and drug free, or I would be discharged. Yes, this therapeutic intervention meant serious business. I wasn't there to play checkers with the other patients, but rather to research the traumatic experiences in my past. To bring them forward to the here and now and face them head on. I was ready. I only needed the reassurance that I would be in good hands. I had to trust others that I would be ok. I had to believe that I could somehow get better by voluntarily entering a Psychiatric Day Program. And I had to trust in myself that I could share my innermost self with complete strangers and the psychiatric staff. I entered this program at the recommendation of my dear friend. I certainly did not have the insight to this on my own.

God, I'm glad there are professional people out there who really give a damn. I trusted her, and I was prepared to do anything to stay clean & sober and become a healthier human being.

Psychiatric Day Program

At this point in my journey I was actually quite excited about the possibility of taking a good long look at me, in an attempt to get to the bottom of what really made me tick. I looked forward to starting this new program, and the therapy it provided. Having never been in a day program like this one, I was also quite anxious.

As I entered the hospital I became ambivalent about my decision. I struggled with inner emotions, which I had suppressed for over twenty years. I could no longer deny their existence. I either plunge forward or retreat back into my old ways. I either continue on this new sober, healthy journey, or I return to the dysfunctional, angry, and violent man I had become.

The feeling of being in a new setting, with new therapists and clients reminded me immediately of all those years in elementary school. Each new school year was fraught with uneasiness and embarrassment. At the beginning of each year I had to make adjustments to a new teacher. Every new class required that I adapt to a new environment. It seemed the harder I tried to fit in, the more I ostracized myself. I was slower than everyone in my class; I could not read like the others, I felt ashamed most of the time, and the harder I tried, the more embarrassment I created for myself. I was always under pressure and stress to measure up.

But this was not elementary school, nor was it public or high school. This was a hospital setting and I was an adult. I was there because I chose to be there. Nobody forced me to apply to this program. I came here on my own free will, and I intended to stay here until such time that I was ready to leave. You see, in every learning situation I had been in I always looked for ways to reinforce that I did <u>not</u> fit in. In this hospital setting I started to search for the reasons why I <u>did</u> fit in. I was open to any learning that I could gain while being here. I wanted to feel better about myself, and this was a very scary and vulnerable place for me to be. I have never handled new challenges very optimistically, so why was this one any different?

I very quickly made friendships with the other patients. I was quite adept at meeting people, and I could adapt to most situations. However I was in a psychiatric day hospital program. This situation was quite different from the streets. I found out early in my treatment that the more I shared with others the closer we became. The closer we became, the more I would open up myself to them. The more I shared with others, the more they reciprocated. I soon realized that I was going to get a lot out of being here. And guess what? I have not touched alcohol or drugs for over a month now. This is the longest period of clean and sober time I have managed to put back-to-back since I started using at age twelve. This is the first time in my 23 years that I was excited to be clean and sober. I wanted so badly to be healthy, but I did not know where this was going to lead me.

The majority of the therapy I was involved in consisted of large and small groups. Large groups consisted of 30-40 people, while smaller groups had 15 – 25 members. There were 1-to-1 counseling sessions with our designated therapist as well. We did groups with video cameras. We worked with our hands in industrial arts shop. I started to make a guitar case for my guitar. We spent a great deal of time sharing our life experiences with each other. As time passed I started to realize that many of the clients seemed to look to me for guidance, support and leadership. We all had very serious emotional and behavioral problems, yet we seemed to form a very strong bond with each other. I was very open about my situation, and soon had other clients leaning on me for support. For the first time ever I started to develop bonds with other people that did not involve alcohol or drugs. For the first time I started to find out what I was really like.

You see it is impossible to hide when you live a clean and sober life. What emerges is the real you. What will come out in this process is the person inside you that has always been there, but was probably hidden just beneath the surface. Finding the real me has been an amazing journey.

I was starting to realize that I wasn't such a bad person after all. I opened my eyes to the possibility that I had a great deal to offer in this world. I had special talents and gifts that I needed to strengthen and develop if I was going to get anywhere in life. Self-discovery is truly an incredible trip. The group that really caught my attention was called "Psycho-Drama". It was scheduled from 12:30pm until 4:30pm each Thursday. It took the full 4 hours to complete a drama. At the beginning of each session the group was asked, "Who would like to do a drama today?" Yeah, each Thursday we were provided with the opportunity to choose a drama about a situation that was traumatic in our lives. Most of us were quiet when asked this, yet instinctively we knew whose turn it really was. In my true avoidance approach to just about anything, I waited, and waited, and waited. The thought of choosing an event in my past and recreating it as if it was happening in the "here and now" was not my idea of a good time. You see, up until now I have mastered many skills to avoid facing these experiences, and now I have chosen a program that focuses on past trauma. I realized that one day it would be my turn, and that I would be faced with the challenge of reviewing my past, or continue running from it. But as long as I can remember I have run from my problems. I remember the promise I made to myself after my dad died that I would never cry, never get angry, and I would never trust another human being – especially adults. I vowed to hurt first before I got hurt. I wanted to control my destiny by any self-destructive means I could find.

Now here I am, 23 years old and in a psychiatric hospital preparing to face my past. And I am not 100% sure that I have what it takes to complete this program. The only option I had was to leave; besides, "I'm a volunteer client – I don't have to be here."

Psycho-Drama

An incredibly gifted therapist facilitated psychodrama. Dr. F. He was skilled at taking a patient through a therapeutic process whereby the individual would recreate a traumatic event in his/her life and act this event out in the present day. It would turn out that this particular group would impact me more than the others. Dr. F. stressed that we take responsibility for our therapy and that he would provide the group with the guidance and direction that we needed. I especially needed this type of direction from a man.

The purpose behind this therapeutic process was to relive a traumatic event in our lives and role-play that episode in the here and now. This required the involvement of other patients who would play key roles in the dramatization. I really learned a lot as a participated in other clients' dramas, and I realized that the time for me to do one was fast approaching.

I remember the particular Thursday afternoon when we entered the group room for our session. By process of elimination I realized that it was probably my turn to do a Psychodrama. As I sat nervously in my seat I waited for Dr. F's invitation for a group member to do a drama. He said, as he always did:

"Who would like to do a psychodrama today?"

He always said this in an inviting, reassuring manner, and today was no exception. I watched the other group members squirm in their seats, trying hard not to make eye contact with Dr. F. But for some unknown reason we locked eyes and he said to me:

"David, how about you?"

I felt an uneasy knot in the center of my gut. My heartbeat increased as adrenaline raced through my veins. I could hear my heart beating inside my ears as I sat dumbfounded for an eternity. I decided that it was time to really work as I rose from my chair and walked toward the center of the group. As I stood up it felt as if my legs would buckle from under me, and I could hear the sighs of relief from the forty or so other patients who were off the hook this afternoon.

Dr. F. supported my decision in a way that only he could. His first question to me was what I would like to do a drama on.

After a long pause I said, "*I would like to work on the loss of my father, Michael.*"

For the next hour and a half we arranged the drama. This involved me sharing, in detail, my recollection of my father's death, from beginning to end. I then went about selecting group members who would participate in the drama by playing significant roles such as my father, my mom, and my two sisters. Once we established these roles Dr. F. had us rehearse the dramatization from beginning to end. It was then we reconstructed the morning that I woke up to learn about my father's death. As we rehearsed, we selected every word that would be said during the drama, right down to the order, the tone of voice, and so on. It was at this point in the drama I realized that I was doubtful whether I could continue or not. I wanted so badly to run out the door, down the hallway, and out into the streets back to my world of pain. I recall shouting out in my head, "STOP, STOP, STOP, I CAN'T DO THIS!"

But something kept me in that room. Something made me stay and stick it out, no matter how painful it was going to be. Maybe it was the trust I had in Dr. F. and his gift of healing. Or maybe it was the support I felt I had from forty or so other group members that were there with me. Or maybe it was because I was tired of always running when things got unbearable. I was sick and tired of being sick and tired. The time had come for me to face the loss of my dad. If I didn't do it now then I would probably have to do it later, and I would continue to let my past dictate how I live today.

I wondered just how much more pain and suffering I had to endure before I was ready to face it. Maybe it was the combination of all of these factors that made me stay in that drama session that afternoon. After all, I'm no quitter. I took pride in the fact that I could follow through with something once I got started. It took every ounce of self-determination I could muster to remain in that room and continue my drama.

What developed over the remaining two hours in group therapy was my return to 62 Standish Avenue in Toronto and to the morning of November 29, 1963. The morning I awoke to hear the sobs from my mom and my two sisters. I re-enacted the long trek to my parents' bedroom door and standing at the foot of my parents' bed. Standing there again I heard the words that my mother spoke:

"Your dad was returning home from Montreal last night and the plane he was in went down in bad weather. He died in the plane crash and will not be coming home. But he would want us to be strong. He is with God now."

Throughout the course of this dramatization all the emotions I had suppressed all these years came flooding to the surface. I felt as if I were the eight-year-old boy who just learned that his father had died. I was overcome with fear, sadness, anger, and loneliness.

All the emotions, thoughts, and memories I had tried to bury all these years were flooding to the surface and staring me in the face. Yes, I was lost, sad, fearful, lonely, and angry from the top of my head to the tips of my toes.

I was so lost in my dramatization and grief that I did not notice that Dr. F. had instructed the other participants to build a wall of pillows and cushions all around me. I was on my hands and knees and my heart pounded, thoughts raced through my head, and I could feel myself ready to explode. For a split second I remembered all the people I had hurt in my life, the classmates I bullied, the fighting, the gang in TO, the self-inflicted wounds, the cross-walk guard, the strappings at school, the early morning walks home from the Wellesley Hospital in bandages, and all the times I had to stuffed my feelings. I thought to myself, I should get up and get the fuck out of here. I don't have to do this. Nobody can make me feel what I don't want to feel. I'm voluntary. The exit is just a few steps away. All I have to do is get up and make a run for the door. Just leave. Just as was preparing to stand up and bolt out the door I heard the only few words that could have helped me to continue.

Dr. F. said, *"David, it is ok to be angry, no one will get hurt."*

His words were the ones I had been waiting to hear for twenty years. No one had ever told me that it was ok to feel mad. No one had ever stopped to guide me through my own emotions. And no one ever said that I am in a safe place to let go of all that inner pain. This is the first time that I was given permission to feel; to feel anger, to feel what I was feeling. All I ever remember hearing is that it was not safe for me to express my anger. That if I did get angry the only way I knew how to be angry was to hurt myself or others. To hit, throw, punch, snort, or drink. No one had actually taken the time to show me how to express my anger. I briefly looked up from the wall of cushions and the man I had selected to be my dad was kneeling on the other side of the wall. I looked at him and saw my father. My father said to me, "David, it's ok to be angry, no one will get hurt." What followed was the release of twenty years of pent up feelings. I punched the pillows, screamed, yelled, and eventually sobbed. I broke through that wall of denial and openly exposed the emotions of a hurt angry child trapped deep within a man's body. My emotions flooded the entire room as I experienced for the first time in twenty years all the pain and anger I had swallowed inside. At the conclusion of my psychodrama I wept for what seemed like an eternity. All my fellow patients had surrounded me and were stroking my head, my shoulders, arms, and back, patting me with a gentleness I had never experienced before in my life. I also recognized the most of our whole group was in tears. Some of us were sobbing – together – sharing our innermost feelings. The comfort I experienced that afternoon I will never forget.

I will forever be grateful to Dr. F. for his special gift. He was instrumental in helping me to trust my feelings and accept support from others in this world. He encouraged me to take the biggest risk I so desperately wanted to take – to trust again. He gave me the permission to be angry at a critical time in my life. He knew what it would take to guide me through the walls of denial I had built up. He supported me at time where I needed the guidance of a trusting male. Thank you Dr. F. I will forever be grateful to you

My time was just about up and I was in the process of being discharged from the Psychiatric Day Program in February 1979. I had spent a fair amount of my time in the company of all these amazing therapists and clients that it wasn't going to be easy to say goodbye. These people had become my family. We shared so much together in the last 7 months. Leaving was beginning to resemble another loss to me.

On my last day, several co-patients and I celebrated in the only manner I knew. We went and got drunk.

I remained drunk for almost five more years. I can never explain to anyone why I deliberately returned to self-destructive behavior. Only another alcoholic or drug addict will understand this. There is no rational explanation for this relapse. I could say that I caught my wife with two other males one night and I lost all sense of reality, or I got caught up in the moment, or better yet, I found it too difficult to really say goodbye. Yet this still does not justify my actions. After all the work I had accomplished I knowingly returned to a lifestyle dictated by alcoholism. This decision would almost bring me to death one more time. This decision would shape my life for years to come. I would create another monster in me that would have to be tamed again. They say that the disease of alcoholism is progressive. Over time this disease will get worse, never better. They say that after a brief period of abstinence from alcohol or drugs that if we use again we will return to where we left off. In a very short period of time we get worse, never better. I am here to say that this is true. My life would get a lot worse before I was able to attempt to sober up again. I was able to return to Child Care Work following my discharge from the hospital program. I re-entered this career after a 9-month reprieve. I felt ready to continue my work with children, even in the midst of a recent relapse into alcohol/drug addiction. I continued to struggle with my addictions and depression. All the work I had accomplished in therapy seemed to have been a waste of time. My disease rapidly worsened, and I eventually progressed into what ended up being my last drunk. I knew that this disease was progressive, yet I had to find out again for myself. You see I thought that my therapy in the hospital program qualified me to drink normally. That with a new relationship, a different job, new friends, a new place to live, I would somehow escape the serious effects of alcoholism. I truly believed that I might be able to handle and control something that I had never had control of before. I desperately wanted to believe that my drinking and drug behavior would mysteriously vanish and I could resume indulging like normal people do. I married for the second time in August 1983 and by December of that same year I almost died.

December 14, 1983 to be exact. I left the Elementary School I worked at, called a taxi, went to the liquor store and a lounge, and proceeded to drink almost 62 oz of my favorite alcoholic beverage in seven hours. I remember the entire evening. I stayed at my friend's home, by myself, for the entire evening, drinking. As I drank I instinctively knew that something very bad was going to happen. I sat, drank as quickly as I could, played records, played guitar, and pretended to be Carlos Santana, imagining what it would be like to be playing at Woodstock in front of 500,000 people. I lived in my make-believe-world all evening. If anyone could have heard the conversations that ran through my head that evening, they would have surely locked me way involuntarily for long time. I fantasized and created so many scenarios in my head about how famous I would be one day. I played the best and worst music I could possibly find that only heightened my emotions. I became more and more depressed and volatile. I was caught between a rock and a hard place. I didn't want to be alone, yet, I'm so glad that no one was around to watch me self-destruct.

My buddy, Al, arrived home to find me completely smashed. More drunk that he ever seen me before. I vaguely recall sitting and talking to him at the dining room table. After what appeared to be a useless one-sided discussion I said "fuck it" and headed down the hallway to a spare bedroom he had. That's when I blacked out for the last time. I regained consciousness at 8:40am, Friday December 15, 1983. I immediately flashed back to the last several minutes after I blacked out the night before. I had reached the spare bedroom, closed the door, and jimmied a chair under the doorknob to secure it closed. I took off my belt and fastened it tightly around my neck. I tried desperately to fasten on to the clothes rack in the bedroom closet. I remember hanging from the clothes rack in the closet for a brief moment and then crashing to my ass on the closet floor.

After a miserable attempt to end my life I staggered a few steps before falling on the bed and passing out immediately.

Like a whirlwind it hit me!

Did I try to kill myself? No fucking way. I can't believe it. I tried to kill myself. What the fuck is wrong with me? I don't want to die. I want to live. I'm not ready to die yet. What's the matter with me? Am I fucking crazy? I don't want to die!

In the very same breath I said the following words: "I need help. I promise I do everything in my power to not drink today."

All day long I was in pain. All day long my head was full of crazy thoughts: **drinking, not drinking, leaving work to get some sleep, getting drunk, suicide, death, grief, pain, sadness, depression.** This was the worst day of my life. I knew I had to do something or I would surely die. I knew I had to stop drinking but I was scared shitless to give it up. Again. I struggled with a conflict in my head as to what to do next. My emotions were all over the place too. One minute I felt fear, then anger, then I would experience extreme sadness, followed always by immense anger. Then back to fear, anger, loneliness, stupidity, shame, guilt, remorse, anger, fear, and sadness. This went on all day.

I didn't know at the time but something or someone had heard my prayer early that morning. "I need help, I promise to do anything in my power to not drink today."

At approximately 6:00pm I phoned Alcoholics Anonymous, and by 8:00pm I was sitting at a meeting with about fifty strangers, drinking coffee and smoking cigarettes. I smelt like a brewery, or someone who might work in one. I also smelt dirty. I was sweating throughout the entire day, and was shaky and extremely nervous at the meeting. I knew that I was partly nervous because of where I was, but I also knew that my shakes were part of the withdrawal from alcohol. I was a total mess. I watched the clock tick by every moment. I knew that only a certain number of people would be asked to share and the closer it got to 9:00pm the less time they would have to ask me to say anything. It was 8:53pm when the chairman looked at the clock and said,

"Looks like we have enough time for one last speaker."

I was probably the one shrinking down to shield myself behind the guy seated next to me.

"How about that young fella seated next the woman in the pink sweater?"

I thought to myself, holy shit – he's pointing at me. What the fuck do I do now? I don't want to speak. I have nothing to say. I know I'll pass, you're allowed to pass. Just then I recalled waking up that morning with a belt around my neck. I also remembered making myself a promise. I WILL DO ANYTHING IN MY POWER TO NOT DRINK TODAY. Well this was definitely in my power. I need to talk because I promised myself I would do anything." I leaned upward and forward in my seat. I took a deep breath and said:

"Hello, my name is David, and I'm an Alcoholic."

I spoke for almost ten minutes and let the entire group know just how fucked up I was, how out of control my drinking had become, how I attempted suicide the night before, and that I needed serious help.

Everyone understood. They greeted me after the meeting. I joined the group and started what would be the most difficult process I would encounter – being sober, one day at a time.

I didn't know then that I had made the right decision to straighten out. It was very, very hard at first, but each day I renewed the promise I had made to myself. If I had known earlier in my life that there was a way out of this mess I would have decided much sooner to sober up. But they told me that you get here when you're supposed to, not a minute earlier. I heard that only alcoholics came to these meetings as normal drinkers never question whether they are alcoholic or not. I heard some of the most honest people share willingly their struggles with life and booze. I had many strangers approach me after the meeting and express how my sharing impacted their recovery. Meanwhile I had no idea what I said. It was only in these rooms where I could find honesty, love, and support. I would leave a given meeting always feeling more hopeful about staying sober than before the meeting started. It was like a drug for me. I always felt connected to someone after a meeting. I would leave the meeting resolved to stay sober one more day. I would go home, climb into bed and stay there until I fell asleep. Oddly enough I would wake up still sober.

What? Me? Native?

Approximately one year before I sobered up for the last time, I was approached and offered a Counseling Position with a newly developed Jr. High School program for Aboriginal students. This program was designed to provide an alternative academic setting for Aboriginal Jr. High School students. Up until this point in my journey I had never been around Native people. My new position would place me smack dab in the middle of native youth, adults, families, and professionals. I started this job with the understanding that I would be providing counseling services for these young people as well as providing them with in-class assistance. When I walked into the school for my first day on the job in the fall of 1982, I noticed that everyone was staring at me. It was as if they could see right through me. I was overcome with the thought that maybe I had made a mistake by coming here, that I didn't belong. It was a very uncomfortable feeling to feel that you do not belong among your own people. But I continued to walk into my new surroundings. I had to believe that I was there for a reason.

I was quickly introduced to the Native culture and began to experience traditional ceremonies for the first time in my life. It opened my eyes to a way of life that was so foreign to me, yet appealing. There was definitely something for me to learn at this school. As fall approached I had the opportunity to participate in a staff retreat in Northern Alberta. As we prepared for this event I realized that I would have to refrain from alcohol for four days before this retreat as we were to participate in a Sweat Lodge Ceremony. I had already learned that if I was drinking alcohol or using drugs I had to abstain for a period of four days before entering this sacred lodge. Meanwhile, I had difficulty putting a couple of sober days back to back, let alone four. I decided that I would follow these new teachings as a sign of respect for this way of life. I accepted that this new learning would require some sacrifice on my part and that it was part of me being Native to prepare myself accordingly. I put my trust in the hands of those people who knew better that I did. I started to accept that I was a Native male and with that came responsibility and expectations. I have since come to understand that many of our people share this experience. Many generations of our people have been removed from our culture and that I was not the only one who experienced the isolation from our way of life. I was somewhat relieved to learn that it was a way of life that I was being taught and not some form of religion.

It was a cold winter day when we set out for our destination, and it was the fourth day that I had not touched alcohol. I was nervous and fearful about the events that were to take place over the next 48 hours. It was sunny and clear outside. Alberta winters can be beautiful. Cold, yes, but beautiful. I have always loved the winter months. I loved being outdoors, playing hockey, skiing, or even tobogganing. The winter bought a certain freshness in the air as it pinched the skin on my face. As a child I recalled winter camping, sliding down huge hills in my snowsuit, and playing shinny hockey until my feet would freeze. Yes I loved winter. The drive to our destination brought back a lot of these memories.

The drive took roughly three hours northwest from Edmonton. I packed accordingly for an overnight stay at the cabin. I had brought with me the specific offerings of tobacco, clothes and a gift for the elder. As we neared our destination I was aware of the fear that was building up inside me. I felt vulnerable, stripped of all my defenses, alcohol, and self-pity. The closer we got to the cabin the more anxious I became.

Naturally, I did not sleep well the night we arrived at the elder's residence. We slept in a round log cabin that was heated only by a wood-burning stove. The comfort the stove provided was indescribable.

When I woke up the next morning I realized that I had been without alcohol for five days now and I felt so strong. I wanted to remain feeling this way forever. We ate a huge breakfast and started to prepare for the sweat lodge ceremony that was scheduled for mid-afternoon.

Again, my emotions started to fluctuate between fear, worry, inadequacy, joy, contentment, then back to worry and fear, and so on.

In the Sweat Lodge, It Felt Like I Returned Home, ...To Saugeen

As I changed into my shorts I realized that I started to feel shaky, unsteady. My nerves started to react to the impending uncertainty. I did not know what to expect and I still did not react well to the unknown. But I continued to prepare, gathering my towel and offerings for the elder. We filed outdoors into the cold sunny winter day. I approached the lodge and awaited instructions. As we entered the lodge my skinny little legs trembled with fear.

"What had I gotten myself into? I don't like small places, I already feel claustrophobic. How long are we going to be in here? I don't think I can handle this. Ah come on David, what's the worst that can happen? So what if it's a little hot in here. You've been in a sauna before. It couldn't be much hotter then that! You agreed to be here. No one is forcing this on you. How are we all going to fit in this little lodge?"

We were all seated in the lodge and the Elder welcomed us all. She seemed like a warm, caring person. I listened to her every word soaking up all the reassurance I could. Then the flaps to the lodge were closed and fear consumed me. It was pitch black and I could already feel the heat from the red hot rocks in the center of the lodge. I remember the Elder saying that if it feels too hot, we could lie down close to Mother Earth where it is a little cooler. But I thought to myself, "I'm tough, I don't need to lay down." But as soon she splashed water on those rocks I hit the ground in a fetal position. Real tough eh!

I tried to focus on the positive as I began to experience this ceremony for the first time.

I thought about my mother Judy, my dad Michael, and all my brothers and sisters. I thought about my biological family; Mina, James, Alice, Kathleen, little Alvin, and all my siblings who I did not know. My head started to flood with so many thoughts. My heart filled with so many emotions from my childhood. The reserve, the loss of all the family I never knew, my mom's death. I started to cry as sweat poured from every pore of my body. I prayed for all my loved ones as I wept like a little child. After four prayers and four songs the round was over and the flaps to the lodge were opened. I was overcome with relief as I thought the ceremony was over. I soon learned that we had finished round one and that we had three more rounds to go. This experience would have an incredible effect on me. As we completed the ceremony I exited the lodge and stood in my bare feet in two feet of snow. Steam was rising from every inch of my body. I felt the most relaxed that I could ever remember. I felt safe. I knew that I had returned to my roots, that I had taken the first of many journeys back to my past, back to Saugeen, to my birthplace, to where all my pain started. Along with the ceremony itself, I learned about the meaning and purpose of the lodge. I felt like a Native young man for the first time in my life. I knew that I would be even more prepared for the next opportunity to sweat. I felt proud of my heritage.

I have come to believe that every Native child, youth, or adult would benefit from this experience. I also understand that other people are welcome to participate in this ceremony, no matter what background they are from. The elders have taught me that this is a "way of living, and it is here for everyone." This teaching fits extremely well for me as I am a product of two cultures, Native and non-Native.

As I continued to struggle with my own unhealthy dependencies on alcohol I was faced with the realization that it would require a tremendous amount of determination and sacrifice to walk this sacred and sober path. My involvement with this school, the students, and the Aboriginal culture was the cornerstone to my search for a healthy lifestyle.

The Long And Winding Road

Admission is the first step toward recovery. A.A.'s first step reads "We admitted that we were powerless over alcohol, that our lives had become unmanageable". Unmanageable, right! My life was a total mess again due to my drinking, and only I can admit that I have a problem. Only I can surrender to the realization that I am powerless over alcohol, no one else can do it for me. It is imperative that the individual wants to stop drinking for themself first. Many times have we attempted to stop for our wife, or the kids, to get a job back, etc. But when we attach conditions to why we stop, then we are likely to return to active addiction. You see the problem drinker has, over the years, not taken responsibility for his/her actions. If they start placing conditions to their behavior, then all is lost. They must want to stop purely because they want to. No other reason is acceptable. Once a condition is placed on a behavior, especially with an addict, then sooner or later he/she will find fault in that condition and return to using. Now, on the other hand, if a person will first view themselves as the only source of the problem then, and only then, are they ready to start taking responsibility for everything that comes with that admission. This is the primary reason why alcoholics return to the bottle. Without anything to blame they are forced, through their own admission, to take a good look at themselves. Many, if not every, alcoholic suffers from an incredibly low self-image to begin with, and having to put in the footwork required to take a hard, honest look at themselves would be enough to send any problem drinker into remission. Their comfort zone is no longer there. You see, when I admit that I am an alcoholic, then I am saying that I am prepared to do anything in my power to stop drinking. I am also admitting that I do not have any excuses to return to alcohol use. I am simply stating that I am ready to take full responsibility for my alcoholic behavior. This includes my feelings, and my actions, my language, my thoughts, my secrets, the wrongs I have done to others and so on. I had used so many excuses for my drinking behavior. It was now time to take on the full responsibility for my drinking behavior. The time for excuses has come to an end. It was time to be as honest as I possibly could about my behavior. The time had come to step up to the plate and enter a lifestyle that was no longer full of excuses to drink. I tried them all. At the time I truly believed that I had a good reason to be out-of-it. But with each episode I came to realize that these excuses were an integral part of my addiction.

Here are just few of my excuses.

I was sad, I was orphaned, I was alone, I lived in so many different homes, nobody cared for me, I forgot I am Aboriginal, nobody understood me, people laughed at me, my dad died, everyone hits me, my mom died, I miss my real family, I feel awkward all the time, I was abused as a child, I was removed from my birth family. I watched my mom die, I hated everything, nothing is fair in this world, I don't belong anywhere, I was angry at the world, I was shy, I was scared, I was full of hate. And so on, and so on . . . I could add a hundred other excuses that alcoholics have used to return to active drinking. Some of these were used to persuade people close to us that we really had no choice but to drink. Even if some of these reasons were true, it doesn't't mean it's all right to drink. Sooner or later the problem drinker will have to face these and many other situations in a sober state.

I would like to caution the reader that once the problem drinker stops drinking, it is only the beginning of their recovery. Don't expect miracles to take shape because recovery never takes shape overnight. An alcoholic has years of self-abusive behavior patterns to untangle. They will likely have years of personal crisis or even traumatic episodes to process. They will require a strict, direct intervention that will include psychological, emotional, physical, spiritual, and medical components. This holistic approach called the Medicine Wheel, only complimented the 12 step program that I had become involved with. A high percentage of recovering alcoholics and addicts cannot handle the recovery process and will return to using the chemical of their choice. This self-destructive relapsing can happen time after time for some individuals. I do not recall all the events that transpired in my early weeks into recovery. I certainly remember fluctuating between being happy and depressed, being on track and being totally lost, having all the answers and forgetting all the questions. But I knew that I was on the right track because I refused to drink. I met some incredibly supportive people in A.A. who really reached out to me when I needed it. They phoned me regularly, picked me up and carried me off to meetings. I started to read about this disease and get involved in my recovery. I remember the following Monday, December 18, 1983 I woke up and realized that, "I didn't have a drink all weekend, that's incredible!" and I felt so very proud of myself – and I knew I was on the right track. I couldn't remember the last weekend that I did not drink or use drugs.

I learned very early in my sobriety that there were concrete actions I could take to improve my resolve to stay clean and sober. I had to strengthen my support, and when I was ready I would commence work on the 12 steps in the program.

The first thing I had to do was eliminate all the drinkers and drug users from my list of friends. Unfortunately, this left me with only a couple of real friends, friends who understood and supported my effort not to drink. The second action I took was to notify everyone in my inner circle that I was not to drink. This shortened my list of friends even more. Thirdly I resolved to attend and participate in as many meetings that I possibly could. At one point in my sobriety I was averaging 20 meetings each week, while working full time with the School Board. Next, I had to select a special person who I felt I could lean on regarding my behavior, and who I would feel comfortable sharing with. Now I was ready to start the recovery process.

The individual I selected became my sponsor. He started to help me do the step work that is suggested in this fellowship. I somehow started to believe that maybe I could sober up and live a half decent life. Yet I had no idea how my resolve to stay clean and sober would be tested many, many times.

I had no inkling of how hard it was going to be to not to resort to my old behavior patterns. I could not have imagined how hard it was going to be to stay sober. But deep down to the core of my spirit, I knew I was going to remain sober.

The Point Of No Return

Within the first three weeks of sobriety I experienced my first days off work without alcohol. My first sober Christmas was two weeks after that, and I was fast approaching my first New Year! What a trip. I was up and down throughout the entire time. I also realized that a small group of friends and I had planned a ski trip to Jasper National Park. This was planned months in advance and as I prepared for this trip I had many serious concerns about going. How was I going to stay sober on a ski trip? Every time I set foot in Jasper I got drunk and high. This would turn out to be my first real test in sobriety. And one I nearly failed.

As we drove to Jasper I could feel myself becoming extremely irritable and withdrawn.

As usual, I was looking for some pity, some sympathy and, in short, an excuse to get shit-faced. I was not taking responsibility for my feelings and actions. By the time we arrived in Jasper I was a walking time bomb. I was a miserable, self-centered little boy, who could not have his way. As we were unpacking I decided to retreat to the bedroom where I could isolate myself form everyone and everything. My wife followed me in shortly afterward and tried to comfort me. I would have none of it. I told her that I was going for a walk to get some fresh air. I left the cabin without saying a word to anyone and slammed the door on the way out. You see, I was a master at eliciting sympathy from people close to me (which is a common characteristic of alcoholics), leaving loved ones to feel guilty and somehow responsible for my actions. I walked out into the cold winter night. With every step I grew more and more self-centered. I was so wrapped up in my own pity that I didn't' even realize that I walked right to the middle of town, which was a good 45 minute trek. I came to an abrupt stop at one the main intersections in town and froze in my tracks. I don't know what made me stop there but I stood staring at the buildings that occupied that particular intersection. I noticed several drinking establishments at this intersection and I began thinking to myself, "Maybe I could just slip quietly into one of these lounges and kick back 4 or 5 doubles. Then I could return to the cabin and everything would be all right. Just a few very quick drinks, as much as possible and as quickly as possible. Nobody would know. Just four or five double shots of Southern Comfort. Mmm how they go down so smoothly, and I know why it's called comfort; because it can remove all the discomfort built up inside, the pain, the anger, the resentments, the self-pity . . . ."

WAIT A MINUTE. Didn't' I make a promise to myself about two weeks ago that I would do anything in my power to stop drinking? Oh crap, I'm so – ------confused!

I was at a crossroads, an impasse; do I or don't I? I don't recall how long I stood at this intersection but I do remember thinking to myself that I had to do something. I couldn't just stand there in the middle of Jasper. It was time to decide. Do I go and have a few quick drinks or don't I?

What I did without even thinking was I closed my eyes and prayed:

"Dear God, I am so lost and confused and I need your guidance. I am an alcoholic and I need help fighting the compulsion to drink. Please help me get through this without drinking."

Tears started streaming from my eyes. I could feel them mixing with the new-fallen snowflakes as they ran down my warm face. It was a tremendous feeling. I was suddenly overcome with thoughts of my dad Michael.

"Dear Dad, I miss you so much and I love you so much. I need you so badly now. Please guide me through this difficult time. If you were standing here with me right now, what would you say to me?"

I shut my eyes and I felt this comforting, warm sensation throughout my entire body. It was the best feeling I had ever experienced in my life. I stood at this intersection for 20 or so minutes before I said to myself:

"Dad would have said 'Don't drink, my son, and get back to that cabin and have some fun with your friends.'".

I was overcome with a feeling of relief. I knew exactly what I had to do. And I was going to do it. First, I was not going to touch a drop of alcohol, and then I was just going to be myself. The obsession to drink was lifted from me.

When I returned to the cabin you could cut the tension with a knife. I couldn't believe how selfish I had been. My friends did not know what to do. They felt helpless, and I contributed to how they were feeling. I looked at them all and said, "Where are the god damn cards, I thought we came out here to have fun!" We played cards until we couldn't play anymore. As we all retired I realized that everyone had fallen asleep except me. Before I drifted off to sleep my thoughts were flooded with several important messages I had heard at the meetings:

"God, Grant me the Serenity
To accept the things I cannot change
Courage to change the things I can
And the Wisdom to know the difference"

One day at a time
First thing's First
Live and let Live
Take it Easy
Keep it Simple
Let go and Let God
Thank you God, and I love you Dad. z.z.z.z.z.z.z.z.z.z

The rest of the trip was a blast. I loved being out on the slope again and I had a renewed confidence that I was doing the right thing by staying clean and sober, and that I had it in me to do it. I returned to work after a two-week break and I knew I was on the right track. I remember I was standing in the main office of our school. All my co-workers were assembling into the office, greeting each other. My supervisor was there in his usual cheerful way. I walked over to him and looked him straight in the eyes and said, "Hey, I haven't touched any alcohol since December 15/83." He looked at me straight in the eyes and said:

"David, I always knew you could do it."

The Beginning of A New Way Of Life

There is one thing that sticks out more than anything else for me in the years that followed; my continual battle with severe depression. I have come to the realization that I will battle with varying levels of depression for many, many years to come. I will always have to accept that I can only do my utmost to manage my feelings in the best way that I possibly can. The key is for me not to view this as a battle, but to learn appropriate ways to manage my feelings, my thoughts, and my actions.

A kind, elderly man told me:

"You need to honor your feelings and experience them. Travel with them for a while, and find a way to release them. The key is to first recognize your inner emotional state and accept that this is part of your journey. Then, allow your emotions to take their course, finally moving on to a place where you can let those emotions go. It's harder than it sounds though."

After finally putting the "plug in the jug" at age 28, I soon realized that I had a lot of pain to process. The meetings were a huge help in identifying the work I needed to do, yet there seemed to always be something missing in my meager existence. But there was one thing was a definite; I could never drink or drug again. Ever.

I entered the New Year of 1984 with a renewed pledge to remain sober. I returned to work and continued to help the youth on my workload. I became more involved in the traditions, values, and ceremonies the school provided, and soon accepted that these teachings could work in parallel with my 12-step program. I realized again that I cannot be satisfied with just one drink or one drug. All my life I could never stop at just one. All my life I needed, and wanted, 20 or more. I had to surrender to the simple fact that once I started, I could not stop.

Within my first six months of sobriety I decided to apply to a Social Work Program at the local Community College. I had very mixed feelings about this decision, as I had not been in a learning environment since the 1972-73 academic year. To my surprise I challenged and passed the entrance exam. This would be the first time since 1973 that I was successful in passing any exam. I was accepted into this Social Worker Program in September 1984, approximately nine months into my sobriety. In the following 12 months I managed to complete the entire first year of the program on a part time basis. By the fall of 1985, I was given time off from my full time job with the School Board to transfer into the second year on a full time basis. This would be the first time I entered a full time academic program for almost 11 years, and believe it or not I was able to handle the academic side of this program. To my surprise, I graduated in the spring of 1986. As I reentered the social work field I continued to struggle with bouts of severe depression, outbursts of anger, suicidal thoughts, low esteem, and generally inner turmoil that would continue to have a choke hold on me. I could not seem to shake the impact of my early years; however I continued to seek answers in the Sweat Lodge, the 12-step programs, and through numerous therapeutic counseling sessions with psychologists.

It was during this part of my life that I was introduced to a barrage of antidepressant medications that provided some relief from my confusion, helped me sleep at nights, and provided some balance for a period of time. Yet there was a constant struggle for me to release suppressed feelings of anger, loneliness, hurt, fear, and guilt. I tried to maintain some degree of sanity in my world by mixing medication, talk-therapy, the 12-step program, and the teachings of the Native Culture. This therapeutic cocktail started to really have an impact on me from time to time. It was following one of my emotional lows that I decided to write to myself. I started out at the beginning and decided to take a chronological review of my life in an attempt to rid myself of the negativity that was still a part of my soul. I still suffered from the good-guy bad-guy syndrome, and it was as if I was still being dragged down by the impact of my childhood years. My life had been a mirage of unpleasant experiences and these memories seemed as if to be part of my daily functioning. I just couldn't seem to rid myself of the negativity that I felt internally. At times it seemed that I would never be able to live a carefree, joyous life. I also became aware of all the many wonderful people I have come into contact with over the years. There are so many I began to feel incredibly grateful for having so many supportive, caring people in my world. For the first time I could remember, I started to place some trust in myself. I began to realize that I had survived life this far and that maybe I was meant to experience the trauma in my life so I could help reach others.

We all need human contact to survive in this crazy world. It is imperative that we have the ability to trust each other. It is also crucial that we have a support network that is aimed at the same result, that being to promote personal and social well being. I have travelled through this world feeling incredibly isolated and alone. It seemed that the harder I tried to fit into this world, the more isolated I felt; the more progress I would make in my therapy, the more steps backward I would slide. The more I began to trust myself in my surroundings, the more vulnerable I felt; the more vulnerable I felt, the harder it was to trust. I wanted so desperately to live in balance with my past, my present, and my future. The need I had to be loved was so strong that I could never be truly satisfied, as I continued to struggle with loving myself – – all of me.

It was during one of my episodes of deep, deep depression that I decided to take a trip to Ontario to research some of my memories. As I was still paranoid of flying I decided to take the bus. I boarded the Greyhound in Edmonton on a Sunday afternoon and four hours later I crossed the Alberta/Saskatchewan border. It was at a rest stop that I realized that if I had flown, I would be in Toronto already. So I hopped back on the bus and decided that I would make the best out of the trip. Boy this was a long drive. The bus stopped at every little hick-town all night long. By late Monday I arrived in Winnipeg, Manitoba. I thought for some reason that we had made good time over night and that we would arrive in TO earlier then they had told us. I could not believe how long it took us to drive through Ontario. But what a drive it was turning out to be. Things started to happen for me the minute we pulled out of Winnipeg and crossed the Manitoba/Ontario border. I could feel it in my heart, but I could never explain what it was. I experienced an internal transformation. I felt it, and it continued to grow as each kilometer passed. I had returned home.

The first stop in was in Kenora, Ontario. A young native male had boarded the bus in Winnipeg, and was seated about three rows ahead of me. I had the whole back seat to myself for the entire trip. As we crossed the border we struck up a conversation. He would eventually join me in the rear of the coach. He was heading back to his reserve in Ontario – Saugeen First Nation, the place of my birth. He was going to meet up with his girl-friend. As he shared part of his story it became apparent that the two of them had a hell of a fight and he was heading back to try and patch things up with her. It sounded as if his drinking had something to do with their quarrels. Now I have always found it easy to talk to other people, even a complete stranger, about their life problems. People just naturally open up to me. As it turned out he was also heading up to Cape Crooker First Nation. This is the reserve where my sisters Kathleen and Alice lived. It turned out that his girlfriend was from Saugeen First Nation. Coincidence? NOT. I don't believe in coincidence. We were put on that bus together for one reason or another. I shared with him that I was from Saugeen and that I was planning to attend their annual Pow Wow in August.

I was aware that something inside me was changing. I sensed that I would never be the same again. I could feel this transformation as it hap-pened. I sat in the back of this Greyhound bus and I knew I would be ok, but it was frightening too. Ontario is such a beautiful province. There is so much to see. The landscape is breathtaking. There are lakes every-where. The bus drove all day and night through this part of northwestern Ontario. I would arrive on downtown Toronto at roughly 3:00pm the next day.

My sister, Claudette, picked me up at the bus depot. She drove me to our home on Standish Avenue in Rosedale. It was unreal to be back home again. I love our home in Toronto. Unfortunately it was a bittersweet return. You see, there was a lot of pain and bad memories at this home. I was flooded by memories of my dad, the spankings, the stress at school, the fights with classmates, the gang years, the drugs and alcohol use, and so on. But it was as if I returned to relive some of this crap so I could move on with my life. My sister showed me some newspaper articles that Mom had kept for all these years regarding Dad's plane crash. This was the first time in thirty odd years that I actually read news accounts of the accident. It was a mind-blower. I was shaking by the time I put the newspaper down, and tears welled in my eyes as I fought to maintain some composure. You see these are the memories and experiences that I struggle with on a daily basis. I decided I was going to explore the neighborhood. I grabbed my wallet, and backpack and headed off down our street, as I had done so many times before.

As I walked down our street I first became aware of all the neighbors we had when we lived there. I could remember most of the family names, and who their children were. I wasn't surprised that almost all of them had moved away. I was flooded with a very powerful array of emotions. I turned the corner at the bottom of the street and headed up Summerville Avenue, just as I had so many times before as a child.

I remember running as fast as I could to get to school on time. I saw the bus stop where I used to catch the bus to get downtown or to a buddy's house. I caught a glimpse at the newspaper boxes at the bus stop and immediately recalled the time when my brother, Steve, Guy, and I tried to cut open the lock on the change box to make a few quick dollars. I also remember that all we accomplished was to bend a very solid pair of wire cutters. I passed my best buddy Steve's place and recalled all the jam sessions we used to have in his basement; just Steve (on drums), Guy (on bass guitar), and myself (on electric guitar). Steve had to do a majority of the singing, as Guy and I were too chicken shit. As I continued up Summerhill Avenue I realized that I was approaching the "T" intersection at Glen Road and Summerhill Avenue. I had to stop. I froze in my tracks. It had been well over thirty years since I ran this specific route at lunch time and stopped to throw mud balls at the cross walk guard. I stood there for what seemed like an eternity. It more likely 15 or so minutes, but it felt like hours. I sat down on the ground beside the elm tree where I picked up the mud balls. I asked myself, "Is there anything I can do to let go of the mistakes I have made?"

I reached into my backpack and pulled out a pouch of tobacco, and one braid of sweet grass. I took some tobacco and sprinkled it around the base of the elm tree. I lit the braid of sweet grass and smudged the tree, the earth, and then myself. I blessed myself by waving the smoke toward my head, my ears, my eyes, my mouth, and finally my heart. As I sat there I closed my eyes and started to pray. It was during this time of prayer that I thanked the Creator for all the Blessings he had provided me with. I thanked him for guiding me toward a life that was free of alcohol and drug use. I thanked him for the opportunity to be raised in such a wonderful community by such loving parents. I thanked him for the precious gift of brothers and sisters, and the blessing of two loving sons.

I then prayed to Creator for forgiveness. I asked that he take care of the elderly man who I had blinded. I asked if there was anything I could do to make this right. I asked for more tolerance and patience to deal with my frustrations, my anger, and my regrets. I then apologized to the man for my actions. I apologized for the pain and suffering I had caused him in a moment of careless and impulsive behavior. I apologized many times before I opened my eyes.

I sat there and cried many tears of regret for the elderly man and I promised that I would never again hurt another human being, as long as I lived.

I continued my journey through my past, visiting my elementary school, The Roman Catholic School where we fought their students, and over to St. Clair Street and Young Streets to my old Senior Public School. All the way I prayed to friends and enemies in my past. All the time asking for forgiveness for the wrongs I had committed.

I ended up walking up Mount Pleasant to the High School where I overdosed on LSD. I prayed to Creator for the teachers I had assaulted and gave thanks for the people who were there for me in times of crisis. I walked all the way downtown to Young and Bloor Streets. This area of the city is where I spent a great deal of time drinking and drugging. I asked Creator for forgiveness for all the times I shoplifted from these stores. I walked all the way to Young and King, recounting all the miserable times I was in these bars.

By the time I reached home, I had walked roughly 20 – 30 miles and looked back at hundreds of life experiences.

I returned home exhausted. I was still very tired the next morning and set out again to explore my past. But before I did I had time to remember the day Dad died. Mom was out for a while, so I took the opportunity to stand at the foot of their bed, just as I had Nov. 29, 1963. I prayed and cried for the loss of my father, and before I left that room I had created a song in my head for his memory.

WHERE DID YOU GO (FOR MY DAD)

Where did you go, when you left me standing here?
Cause I didn't know, if you were far or near
Where did you go, when you left me standing here?
Where did you go, daddy dear?

Where did you go? "63" was a real bad year
And I couldn't show, the pain behind the fear
Where did you go, when you left me standing here?
Where did you go, daddy dear?

I loved you so, you meant the world to me
But my world fell apart, and I couldn't see
That it was nobody's fault, I put the blame on me
Cause I was too young to see

Where did you go, when you left me standing here?
Cause I didn't know, if you were far or near
Where did you go, when you left me standing here?
Where did you go, daddy dear

(spoken)
The years fly past so quickly it seems
And I've prayed constantly
And I've had to find a way
To set my daddy free
He's always in my heart
That's the way it's meant to be
His spirit is always a part of me

I know where you go, when you left me daddy dear
Although I can't see you, I know that you can hear
So there's just one more thing
Let me make this perfectly clear
I Love you so much daddy dear
I Love you so much daddy dear
And I miss you so much, daddy dear

Word & Music By
David Languedoc
"Thunder Voice"

Form 34

MEDICAL CERTIFICATE OF DEATH
OF AN INDIAN

(For use of Registrar-General only)

PROVINCE OF ONTARIO

NAME OF INDIAN AGENCY TO
WHICH DECEASED BELONGED ....

1. PLACE OF DEATH:

(1) If on a Reserve ....

(Give name and locality)

(2) If in a City, Town or Village ....

(State name)

Street Address ....

(If death took place in a hospital or other institution, state the name thereof)

Township of .... County or Territorial District of ....

(3) If in a rural area ....

(State name and post-office address)

Township of .... County or Territorial District of ....

2. PRINT FULL NAME OF DECEASED   P E T O N O D U O T (Surname)   J A N E 2 (Given names)

3. DATE OF DEATH July 26 55 (Month by number) (Day) (Year)   **4. SEX OF DECEASED** M (State whether male or female)

5. CAUSE OF DEATH (Read carefully the instructions on the reverse side)		DURATION		
		Years	Months	Days
GROUP 1				
IMMEDIATE CAUSE. State the disease, injury or complication which caused death, not the mode of dying, such as heart failure, asphyxia, asthenia, et cetera.	(a) congestive heart failure due to (b)			
MORBID CONDITIONS, if any, giving rise to immediate cause (state in order backwards from immediate cause).	due to (c)			
GROUP 2				
OTHER MORBID CONDITIONS (if important) contributing to death but not causally related to immediate cause.	Senility			

6. (1) IF DEATH WAS A FEMALE, WAS THE DEATH ASSOCIATED WITH PREGNANCY? no (Yes or No)   (2) DURATION OF PREGNANCY .... WEEKS   (3) WAS THERE A DELIVERY? .... (Yes or No)

7. (1) WAS THERE A SURGICAL OPERATION? no (Yes or No)   (2) DATE OF OPERATION .... (Month by number) (Day) (Year)   (3) STATE FINDINGS ....

8. (1) WAS THERE AN AUTOPSY? no (Yes or No)   (2) STATE FINDINGS ....

9. IF DEATH WAS DUE TO VIOLENCE STATE WHETHER IT WAS AN ACCIDENT, SUICIDE OR HOMICIDE .... DATE OF INJURY .... (Month by number) (Day) (Year)

STATE HOW THE INJURY WAS SUSTAINED ....

STATE NATURE OF INJURY ....

STATE WHETHER INJURY TOOK PLACE AT HOME, IN INDUSTRY, OR IN A PUBLIC PLACE ....

I certify that,—

(a) I attended the deceased from the 26 day of July , 1955 to the 26 day of July , 19 55 that inclusive,

(b) I last saw the deceased alive on the .... day of .... , 19 .... ; and

July 26 55
(Month) (Day) (Year)

(Address of doctor)
Rat Elgin
Ont

(Physicians who are medical practitioners only, or medical officer of health)
M.D.

(To be used by division registrar only)

REGISTRATION NUMBER ....

I am satisfied as to the correctness and sufficiency of this medical certificate and the statement of death, and I register the death by signing the certificate and statement this .... (Month by number) (Day) (Year)

(Signature of division registrar)

(Code number)

Form 30

PROVINCE OF ONTARIO
THE VITAL STATISTICS ACT

STATEMENT OF BIRTH
OF AN INDIAN

(For use of Registrar-General only)

PROVINCE OF ONTARIO   NAME OF INDIAN AGENCY
                           IN WHICH BIRTH TOOK PLACE _____ *Sturgeon*

1. PLACE OF BIRTH:
   (1) If on a Reserve _____
                                        (State name and location)
   (2) If in a City, Town or Village _____ *New Langston*
                                        (State name)
   Street Address _____
                                        (If birth took place in a hospital or other institution, state the name thereof)
   Township of _____ County or Territorial District of _____
   (3) If in rural area _____
                                        (State name and post-office address)
   Township of _____ County or Territorial District of _____

2. PRINT NAME OF | P | E | T | N | L | O | Q | d | o | T | | | | | | | | |
   CHILD IN FULL: (Surname)
                        | A | L | F | R | E | D | | | | | | | | | | | | |
                                        (Given names)

3. SEX _____ 4. DATE OF BIRTH _____ *June 5, 1955*
   (Write male or female)   (Month by name)   (Day)   (Year)

5. (1) Single [X] Twin [ ] Triplet [ ] Other [ ]   (2) If "OTHER" state the number _____
       (Place X in the proper square)
   (3) If a twin, triplet or other, state whether the child was born first, second, third, et cetera _____

6. THE MOTHER OF THE CHILD IS: SINGLE [ ]   MARRIED [X]   WIDOWED [ ]   DIVORCED [ ]
                                        (Place X in the proper square)

7. WAS THE BIRTH PREMATURE? _____   8. IF PREMATURE STATE LENGTH
                            (Yes or No)   OF PREGNANCY IN WEEKS _____

Husband   MOTHER
(Before completing items 9 to 14, both inclusive, read note 1)

9. PRINT _____ *Petnaquot*   15. PRINT _____ *Mactwas*
   NAME   (Surname)   MAIDEN   (Maiden surname)
              _____ *Harley*   NAME   _____ *Mina*
                (Given names)   (Given names)

10. BAND OR TRIBE _____ *Chippewas Sturgeon*   16. BAND OR TRIBE _____ *Chippewas Sarge*
11. RESIDENCE _____ *New Post*   17. RESIDENCE _____ *Langston Res*
       (If on a Reserve, state name and location)   (If on a Reserve, state name and location)
12. PLACE OF BIRTH _____ *Ont*   18. PLACE OF BIRTH _____ *Ont*
       (Province or Country)   (Province or Country)
13. AGE LAST BIRTHDAY _____ *28* YEARS   19. AGE LAST BIRTHDAY _____ YEARS
14. (1) TRADE, PROFESSION OR _____ *At home*   20. (1) TRADE, PROFESSION OR _____ *Housewife*
       KIND OF WORK   (See note 2)   KIND OF WORK   (See note 4)
    (2) TYPE OF INDUSTRY _____   (2) TYPE OF INDUSTRY _____ *At home*
        OR BUSINESS   OR BUSINESS
                   (See note 3)   (See note 5)

21. HOW MANY CHILDREN BORN TO THIS MOTHER BEFORE THIS BIRTH:
    (a) were born alive? _____ *6*   (b) are now living? _____ *6*
    (c) were born dead after the mother was pregnant at least 28 weeks? _____

22. MEDICAL PRACTITIONER OR | M | c | I | T | B | H | M | | | | | | | | | | | |
    NURSE IN ATTENDANCE   (Signature)
    AT THIS BIRTH | D | R | | | L | E | S | L | I | E | | | | | | | |
                                        (Given name or initials)
                             _____ *New Langston, Ont*
                                        (Post-office address)
                                        (See note 6)

I CERTIFY THAT TO THE BEST OF MY KNOWLEDGE AND BELIEF ITEMS 1 TO 22, BOTH INCLUSIVE,
ARE TRUE AND CORRECT.
                                                   June   1955
                                               (Month by name) (Day) (Year)
_____ *Langston Res*   _____ *Mrs Mina Petnaquot*
(Post-office address)   (Signature)

                                        (This space for use of division registrar only)

REGISTRATION NUMBER _____ *15-55*

I am satisfied as to the correctness and sufficiency of this statement and register the birth by signing the statement this
_____
(Month by name) (Day) (Year)
_____ *Code 33*
(Code number)   (Signature of division registrar)

9008-7-1
1N-5-55

104   David Alfie Languedoc

RE: ...., Alfred, Indian,
born June 6, 1965, Protestant
........., Bernard, Indian,
born January 6, 201., Protestant

Mother — Nina, born April 14, 1917. Indian deaf mute of the Six Nation Reserve. She attended the Belleville School for the Deaf. She is described as a pleasant, easy going person who brought a great deal of her children and took good care of them when they were young. She married James Betsamosad, an Ojibway Indian and there were eight children. Alfred and Bernard's mother was killed on May 20th, 1.6., when a car jumped the ... on the highway and .. through the Reserve. The driver was charged with negligence.

Mrs. ....'s parents were Charles and Mary Martin. Mr. Martin was born on the Six Nation Reserve. Mrs. Martin .... first on .... (......).

In .... to ... that the death of Bernard's adopted father constitutes the second time that he has lost a parent by accidental death. .. was four years old when his ... died and our file indicates that he was with his mother at that time.

About the Indian background, we would suggest that Mr. .... contact with the Indian Centre on Church Street, Toronto. They have information ... on the different tribes and their history.

A Mother's Story

In her cover letter, of which I only have a rough draft that may or may not be what she actually sent, this is what she says.

> *Dear Sir,*
>
> *I have written the enclosed from experience and from the heart! What it lacks in literary value I hope it makes up for in content.*
>
> *If you find you can't use it I would appreciate your sending it back to me. It is my first effort in writing and although it might not make your magazine I'm sure my children would be interest in reading it when they are older.*

So now we are older and here it is!

Saugeen First Nation - 2014
Still Searching For Mom.

Saugeen First Nation - 1978
Identified as my birth home by a community Elder

Tragedy surrounds us daily: Thank God we feel it will never happen to us! Or was I unusual in my complete and utter confidence in the goodness and joy of my life. I was brought up with love – love of God – parents, brother, friends – Sorrow had yet to touch me. Probably the only disappointment was never to make the grade as a great actress which I always felt I was. But what was success on the stage compared to a husband I adored and three adorable children.

Then one day my whole delightful world collapsed around me. My only son four years old, drowned beside me. I didn't even know he was there! Claudette, his six year old sister, saw his fishing rod floating near the dock, looking below was my son Desmond. Immediately, I dived in got him on the dock and began artificial respiration, it seemed days before more help came, but all to no avail. Six hours later they told us our son was dead.

I felt I was dead myself and wished I were. How could I possibly live without my son? The funeral was over and I was surrounded by my heartbroken husband, parents and friends - and they were heartbroken for Desmond had left each one with some of his own special warmth. He had such empathy and joy of life that no matter who he came in contact with some of his magic charm would lighten their own life. I hope I don't write this as a prejudiced mother. For I know to every mother each child is very special in their own special way. But I'm writing this not only   from my own belief but from the hundreds of letters I received who told me what their knowing Desmond had meant to them.

So many friends would say "How wonderful for you to have your religion, what a help it must be." Help? It was torture! How easy to believe when everything is wonderful, naturally this must be a loving God. But now everything wasn't wonderful and all the endless debates that I remembered about God – raging because some of my nicest friends couldn't accept God, heaven came back to me.

Maybe they were right and I was wrong! I didn't want to believe because it comforted me. I wanted to believe because I knew it was so. If there was a God then Desmond would be happier with him than we could ever make him. A hundred years from now we'll all be dead and we'll all be together. All these thoughts and many others haunted me. I could think of nothing else. My husband was the pillar of strength. He who had never accepted anything without questions and doubts especially his religion – yet he knew that God wanted Desmond. He had served his purpose and he thanked God for the four full and perfect years we had him with us. Claudette who was so especially close to her brother, dressed alike, shared the same room, missed him desperately, but was so happy for him. One day we were down in the cellar getting out the ice skates – there were Desmonds with his little red socks tucked inside - I dissolved on the spot – a little hand crept around me and a surprised but sympathetic voice said, "Don't cry Mummy, you know heaven is much nicer than here and there is even a bigger and better skating rink which God will let Desmond play on." We had two dogs, on died, Claudette explained how fair God must be to share - now we have one dog and Desmond has the other. The baby Michelle was too young to understand but how with such faith surrounding me could I doubt? Do I wallow in self pity and let others carry on? Sometimes it was so tempting – carrying on seemed such an effort, but when it came right down to it I had no choice – I had to carry on, for the sake of all those around me. While putting up the brave front I prayed, read and studied anew not just my Anglican Faith, but all Faiths – When months later someone sent me these lines –

"Your son is not dead.

He is more alive than ever.

Each of us has a rendez-vous with death. Life is the childhood of immortality."

Quoted from I know not where I didn't think – I knew it was so.

Now I had finally come to terms with my faith, grateful and more humble.

Realizing that is I had lost my faith I'd have lost my son forever. By keeping my faith my son will never be lost.

He is still very much part of out family and because of him our family is now much larger. We felt we could like to do something very special for our son and knew that the nicest thing we could do would for him would be to give a child a home that would otherwise not have one. We didn't mean a small fair headed, blue eyed baby which thousands of parents are anxiously waiting for daily, but a child classed as "Unadoptable". After a visit to The Children's Aid we found that there were three that went under that catalogue, the mentally handicapped, the physically handicapped and a coloured child. Due to a limited income we felt we couldn't cope with the first two but certainly the latter held no such problem. I will spare you all the red tape we went through but six months later we had two more sons. We had no intention of taking two boys but we'd never separate brothers! WE took them sight and picture unseen and that alone is a story in itself. I already felt those first five minutes would be the most tender of my life. We would hold our arms out and then two poor unloved children would melt gratefully into them. Tears would come to my eyes as I visualized this tender scene. Little did I know how wrong I was! Into a very bleak room were called two bleaker little boys, they stood as if frozen and gazed at us with sullen black eyes as if saying, "and just who are you?" Knowing their past and their many many homes I could understand their distrust but was disappointed at this obvious lack of enthusiasm. Once out of the Waiting Home and into the car I felt a little of the tension leave and knew now was the time I must broach the subject of names. I had been warned by all good meaning or otherwise, on all the emotional problems we were to expect in adopting older boys – four and five who had had such a disturbed life. If this were true I felt I would add one more and choose names we loves. With all due apologies for those who like the names we frankly hated the sound of Bertrum and Albert.

I explained to them that when I met their Daddy I changed my name and added then when we have our children we also chose their name. This fascinating bit of news was greeted with two solemn "oh". Not discouraged I asked if they would like to be called "Andre" and one "Jacque?" Getting no response at all then said, "What about David or Jeffrey?" The youngest one gave his first grin and said "Davin?"All but shouting with glee I blurted out, "Good for you, you'll be David and you'll be Jeffrey. In the weeks that followed one or the other might forget and say, "Albert or Bertrum", then gales of laughter would follow with, "Who's he? I don't know him!"

Naturally all problems weren't settled so quickly or happily. They were emotionally and mentally starved, they didn't know the colour of the sky or the grass. Who God was or even Santa Claus was – How to count to two or any of the things we take for granted. The only thing they did know well was to fight, the dirtier the better. This amazed my daughters but through the months to come the boys learned fair play. Claudette learned to hold her own and Michelle now two because as tough as the boys which was good for her as in the past year been the only one at home during the day it was awfully hard not to baby and probably over protect her. Although they were brothers their personalities were completely opposite. David was outgoing, funloving enthusiastic - once the hitting and lying problem was solved it was hard to believe David had ever lived anywhere else.

Jeffrey being older and an introvert found it much harder to accept that he really was part of out family for ever and ever. His negative manner we found the hardest to cope with. I tried to discipline as little as possible but when it became necessary to remover Jeffrey to his room he would always shout, "I hate you: you hate me." At times I'd think to myself, "you're so right," but I would hug him and say how sorry I was he hated me when I loved him so much. Soon love and patience finally won out. He stopped asking, "Are you really going to keep us?" "Are you never going to send us back to awful places?" When discipline had to be used no dramatic emotional scenes followed. He too had become part of out family for ever and ever.

Prejudice is only found in adult so naturally our children who by the way are Canadian Indians, have become part and a popular part of "the gang" on the street. In the summer when they found their mother spending any spare moments trying to get a good tan were so smug when I told them that God had given them a head start and we were all jealous of their lovely brown skin.

After Xmas they will have a new baby and instead of guessing whether it's going to be a girls or boy they feel my tummy and grin delightly saying, "I bet it comes out with a tan like ours."

Two years have passed since we lost our Desmond. The ache inside never lessons but we've learned to live with it. Thanks to Desmond who is closer to us now then ever before we have had this rewarding experience in bringing these two brothers into out home and hearts.

How I pray for all those adults who say, "if only we could have children," would do something about all those children who cry out for their own Mummy and Daddy. If at first they took a child only for the child's sake they would soon know that their own happiness would double in the joy and satisfaction of seeing their chosen child discover the wonder of God's happy safe and loving world.

And for those parents who have lost a child, what better memorial could you give him than to give another child a home that otherwise wouldn't have a home.

For your sake may you turn your sorrow into a joy for others. How proud he'll be. I know Desmond is.

Judy Languedoc

It was during this trip to Toronto that many changes started to emerge inside my soul. I started to remember some of the most fantastic times in my whole life. Although I was a violent, angry, and lonely child and teen, there were many fantastic times during these years.

"All you need is love, love
Love is all you need."

All You Need Is Love
Lyrics & Music By:
J. Lennon & P. McCartney

I remember always being impacted by love from others starting with my mom and dad. They were the two people who made the decision to save me from a life of misery. They were the only ones who could touch my heart and offer hope to me at a time when I had lost all hope. They demonstrated through their words and actions that I too could become a loving, caring human being. They taught me that I had the capacity to accept love from others in this world and allowed me to grow and learn from my mistakes. Mom and dad are truly "angels on earth" as their love and support were the crucial element in my recovery.

I decided to return to my home reserve for the Annual Pow Wow. I arrived at Southampton, Ontario, and stood on the Pow Wow grounds. It felt as though my feet were glued to the earth as the beat of the Grandfather Drum played. I closed my eyes and cried. This was the first time I had returned to my roots clean and sober. I felt the wind blowing in my face as the beat of the drum traveled through the ground, into my feet, up my legs and right into my heart. I knew I was home, but what I didn't know was how god damn hard it was going to be to return to Alberta. I wanted to stay. I wanted to sleep right there on the ground. I wanted to stay until all the anger and fear was washed from my soul. I wasn't ready to return to Alberta. But I knew I must.

After returning to Edmonton, Alberta, I succumbed to a deep dark depression. I attempted to work and help raise my two sons, but every day was a hurdle. I stopped eating, and lost many pounds. I would either sleep all the time or not sleep enough. I entered one of the darkest depressions I had ever experienced. My outbursts could be triggered by the smallest event or memory. I continued to experience an internal battle between the good-guy and the bad-guy conflict I have had with myself for as long as I could remember.

HOW CAN YOU MEND A BROKEN HEART

"How can you mend a broken man?
How can a loser ever win?
Please help me mend my broken heart
And let me live again."

How Can You Mend A Broken Heart
Lyrics & Music By:
The Bee Gees

Anyone whose heart has been broken repeatedly will know how hard it is to repair an injured heart. It almost feels as if it will never mend. Life and all its beauty does not totally repair the damage that has been done. Time and a great deal of support will always help, yet I have always been under the belief that my pain will never ever go away entirely. As my life seemed to be improving on the outside, the inner turmoil and confusion was not leaving me. For me it seemed as though I would always take two steps forward and three back. I should have just continued to take one step back.

As corny as it may sound, love is what makes the world go round. Love is the most powerful emotion known. Love for self and for others is what we all are searching for. Some people are lucky enough to find true love. Others are not as fortunate. Love is the force that can bring all people together. Love is stronger that anger. Love can touch all people, and can even stop wars. When love is expressed it creates a life-long connection between people. Love is the catalyst for change. If someone feels loved they will likely do anything to experience this emotion again. If an individual does not experience love then they will walk through life searching for it. Love comes from, and goes directly to the heart. Although we are from different backgrounds, different cultures, our hearts are the same color. Elders teach us that they longest journey we will make in life is from your head to your heart. Then, and only then, will you feel complete and in balance. This journey can take a lifetime. Others have been taught that the intellect should rule the emotions. Yet when it comes to love, nothing is more powerful. The key to true happiness is a balance between the head and the heart.

I have experienced love time and time again in my life. During this time it has been love that keeps pulling me back from the inner darkness I experience. At times I still find what little reserve I could muster to combat the trauma I experienced. There were times where it would have been easier just to lock myself away in that dark place and resign myself to a living hell. There were many times when I gave up and believed that I would live a life ruled by pain and anger. But it was love that would always draw me back.

I have been told that you cannot take anyone somewhere that you have not been yourself. Therefore, I understand that in order to love another you must first find a way to love yourself. How can you give what you don't have? Love for self is by far the most difficult love to truly capture and keep for some of us. The only thing that interferes with self love is the impact of life experiences. To anyone who is out there and struggling to feel self love, all you have to do is reach deep inside yourself and determine when and how the love for yourself was impaired. Then you have the power to re-love yourself. You will need the safety and comfort of many supports, which I know are out there. Once these are in place, it is really up to you how hard you work to achieve self-love. It seems that the harder one works will directly impact the quality of learning one receives. Believe me. I did it the long, hard way and it took me a long time to find true love for myself.

I could not continue to write this without acknowledging some very important people in my world. These two individuals have supported my quest for love, and I will continue to attempt to express my gratitude to them.

My sons have been an amazing part of my development into manhood. I was blessed with their births, and the role I entered as their father. We have experienced fabulous times together. They taught me so much about myself and they brought out in me the true meaning of being a man and a father. Even in times when I struggled with my role as a dad, they were a source of pride and joy that only a son can give to a dad. To have a son that you love totally is a gift; to have two sons that you would do anything for is truly a blessing. I could write an entire volume on being a father.

TO JOSH: BORN APRIL 18, 1987

My son, you are everything I prayed for in a son.
You are Kind, Respectful, Intelligent and Creative.
I've loved you since the first time I set eyes on you.
I will continue to love you forever.
You are the young man that I have always wanted to be.
I wish I could be like you when I was a younger.
Thank you for being you.
I am so proud of the young man that you are.

TO CHRIS: BORN DECEMBER 28, 1989

My son, you completed our family
On the day you were born.
I love you because you are such a Sensitive,
Caring, Respectful and Intelligent man.
You have touched my heart with you kind and gentle nature.
I have loved you since the first time I saw you.
And I will love you forever.
Thank you for being you.
I am so proud of the young man you are.

FATHER & SON

(Father):
It's not time to make a change, just relax and take it easy
You're still young, that's your fault, there's so much you have to know
Find a girl, settle down, if you want you can marry
Look at me I am old, but I'm happy

I was once like you are now and I know that it's not easy
To be calm when you've found something going on
So take your time, think a lot, why think of everything you've got
For you will still be here tomorrow, but your dreams may not

(Son):
How can I try to explain, when I do he turns away again
It has always been the same, same old story
From the moment I could talk, I was ordered to listen
There's a way and I know that I have to go away, I know I have to go

(Father):
It's not time to make a change, just sit down and take it slowly
You're still young, that's your fault, there's so for you to go through

Find a girl, settle down, if you want you can marry
Look at me I am old, but I'm happy

(Son):
All the times that I cried, keeping all the things I knew insider
It's hard, but it's harder to ignore it
If they were right, I'd agree, but it's them they know not me, now
There's a way and I know that I have to go away, I know I have to go.

Father & Son
Words & Music By:
Cat Stevens

What
It's
Like
Now!

By the time this book is complete I will have been married to my third wife Marcie, for over six years. I am so grateful for Marcie coming into my life following the separation from my son's mother. Marcie is everything I've ever wanted in a partner. We do everything together. It feels like we have known each other all our lives. We share so much in common. One of the most precious gifts we share is sobriety – yes, neither one of us drinks alcohol or takes drugs. Our connection to each other is pure and clean. We both want to live a clean and sober lifestyle. I have never experienced this kind of relationship where everything is so real. Marcie and I have traveled through a lot in a short period of time together. I have truly learned to give unconditionally. She has brought into my life all that I wanted in this world – a partner, a friend, a lover, a companion, a music partner, trust, honesty, and unconditional love. Today I have all I want and need in this world – two amazing sons, three step-children, four fantastic foster children, a beautiful partner, a roof over my head, a career that I love, the support of many, many friends, recovery, a Higher Power, a 12 step program, culture, identity, love, self-worth, musical talent, the ability to be creative. Today I know what self-love is. Today I choose to be free of my past. Today I enjoy all the hard work I have put into becoming a caring human being. Today I love myself, and all those who are close to me. I appreciate life more today than ever. I want to be remembered as a gentleman, not an angry bully. I want to give and get the most of what this world has to offer. I choose today to forgive all the harm that was done to me, and get on with living life to the fullest. I have also forgiven myself for all the wrongs I have caused others. Marcie and I were married September 27, 2008 in a beautiful non-alcohol event, surrounded by family and friends. We have gone on to complete all the training required to become Foster Parents. We have been blessed with caring for almost a dozen different children, one of which we are in the process of adopting. This is truly a gift from the Creator.

I would not be the person I am if it had not been for James Petonoquot, Mina Martin, Michael Languedoc, Judith Languedoc, 18 Foster Homes, The Orphanage, all my natural siblings, Claudette, Jeff, Michelle and Sean, my teachers, my principals, all my friends growing up, Seneca College in Toronto, John Brown Jr. and all the amazing co-workers I met early in my career, all the incredible professional workers in Child Care and Social Work, Dr. Frank and all the therapists at the Aberhart Psychiatric Day Program, Alcoholics Anonymous, Narcotics Anonymous, and all my friends in these fellowships, all the therapists (to many to recount), my beautiful sons Josh and Chris, my loving partner Marcie and her children.

I have known for some time that someday I would reach a point when I could honestly say at last I am free. At last I can be me, at last all the pain is gone. Now I can live life to the fullest.

WOMAN I KNOW...

"Woman, I know you understand
The little child inside the man"

"so let me tell you again and again and again
I love you, yea yea now and forever"

Woman
Music & Lyrics By:
John Lennon

As my life moves forward I have spent a great deal of time teaching others about my journey, through work, guest speaking, daily living, and music. The following pages are original songs and poems that I have created during my 30 years of sobriety that inspired me. I hope they do the same for you.

FOR ALL OUR CHILDREN

There are so many broken spirits
The joy they felt has turned to pain
Their dreams are shattered, their tears unwept
By promises that were made but never kept

Children today are full of fear
By all they see and what they hear
They learn that life is one big secret
Not knowing who to trust or who will care

Reach to the child within us all
For change must first come from within
The cycle of abuse must be broken
So healing for all our children can begin

It's time to reach into their sadness
It's time to end their misery
Let's give hope to all our children
That maybe someday, they'll be free

Reach to the child within us all
For change must first come from within
The cycle of abuse must be broken

So healing for all our children can begin

It's time to reach into our sadness
It's time to end all misery
Let's give hope to all our children
That maybe someday, they'll be free

Words & Music By
David Languedoc
Thunder Voice

ALFIE'S SONG

Ever since he was a little guy, all he saw was clouds in the sky
And it would finally clear up, just to rain again
He was taken from his family, a little boy no more than three
Life would never be the same, Alfie was his name
Eighteen different homes tried to give, little Alfie a place to live
But every time that he would leave, more rejection he would perceive
The Orphanage became his mom and dad, he was full of fear and very sad
He always thought he'd done something wrong, to feel this way so long

Life just isn't fair, why can no one care?
Nobody could really show, little Alfie how to grow

He was adopted at the age of four, a moved from his home by the shore
He ended up in the city, where he lost his identity
He grew up tough and he grew up mean, he was confused by all he'd seen
And by the time that he was eight, a plane crash sealed his fate
When they told that his father died, he was sure that everyone lied
But he made himself a promise, and one he planned to keep
He started glue and drinking alcohol, it made him feel like he was ten feet tall
And from one bottle to another, he'd soon fall fast asleep

Life just isn't fair, why can no one care
No one could really show, little Alfie how to grow

He spun his wheels till he was twenty-eight, but my friends it's never too late
To let the healing start, and to wash away the pain
For love, respect and honesty, combined together will set you free
Little Alfie's living proof, there're people around who'll care
So take from someone who knows, face your pain and your spirit grows
For we can break this cycle, and set our children free
Let nothing get in your way, of feeling stronger each and every day
Please remember you're not alone, there're people around who'll share

Maybe life's not fair, it's up to us to care
It's up to use to show other Alfies' how to grow

Ever since he was a little guy, all he saw was clouds in the sky
He was taken from his family, a little boy no more than three
Life will never be the same
Alfie is my name

Words & Music by
David Languedoc
"Thunder Voice"

LOVE WILL CONQUER ALL

A little child knows love at first, a gentle hug quenches his thirst
He feels accepted, he is loved
But he's thrust into a world of pain, he hurts all over, again and again
His little world comes crashing down

What's kept inside can't help tomorrow
Hanging on to pain and sorrow
All the happy times remain a misty river in my brain
Covered in the morning dew, and vanish when the sun shines through
I reach for them but when I'm near, they disappear

A loving family steps in to care, a mother and a father who's always there
They try to guide him to a better way of life
But tragedy strikes, his father dies, he thinks the world is full of lies
An buries himself deep within his pain

What's kept inside can't help tomorrow if I hang on to pain and sorrow
All the happy times remain, a misty river in my brain
Covered in the morning dew, and vanish when the sun shines through
I reach for them but when I'm near, they disappear

But love will triumph in the end, His little heart is on the mend
As he searches for his place in this world
Support and kindness from a friend, unconditional love right to the end
It's time to release the demons of his past

What's kept inside can't help tomorrow
If we hang on to pain and sorrow
Let all the happy times remain
That misty memory in my brain
I'll count my blessing each and everyday
Take a stand and let me hear you say
That only love can conquer all

Words & Music By:
David Languedoc
"Thunder Voice '

Everywhere I go in this hectic world I am continually reminded that the world is packed with loving, caring people. I meet them on the street, in my work, in our schools, in church or at a ceremony. I speak to them on the phone or at a restaurant. They are everywhere. They are our neighbors, our friends, in our families. Everywhere you turn there is a loving, caring human being. So I ask myself, "With all these loving people around, then why is this world in such a mess? Why is it that the negative forces get all the attention? How come every time you turn on the TV or the radio there is more bad news? Why are we drawn toward negativity? What is it that makes us pay to see a fight at a hockey game? What is so appealing about violence and negativity? Why does it sell as well as is does? Why is mankind fixated on the pain of their fellow man? Why? Why? Why? Why is the almighty dollar more important that the future of the entire planet?" There is something very wrong with this picture.

TAKE MY AND SHARE THIS LAND

"Take my and share this land,
There's room enough for everyone."

The Way It Used To Be
Music and Lyrics By:
David Languedoc
"Thunder Voice'

As I continued to mature emotionally I found another strength in my recovery. I started to write music that helped me release and process my pain. I realized again that Dad had also left me not only with a passion for music, but a skill that could help me heal. I fell asleep one night at midnight. I awoke abruptly with these words echoing in my brain. I sat up and repeated them to myself, and I immediately realized that these word fit perfectly to a piece of music I had created years before. As I sat in my bed I said to myself:

"THE WAY IT USED TO BE"

There used to be, a world that's free, of pain and isolation
When people shared, and showed they cared – That's the way it used to be

The world has changed, people seem strange – there's far too much
separation
The anger's real, and the pain we feel – has changed the way it used to be

We all should live, and learn to give – Let's unite as one
Take my hand, and share this land – There's room enough for everyone

But until then, I'll cry again – And pray we come together
I won't despair, I'll meet you there – Back to the way it used to be

Words and Lyrics By
David Languedoc
'Thunder Voice

You see, I need to believe that there is a power "greater than myself" which oversees all of mankind. I know that we all share in a belief; it's just that we choose to practice our own beliefs in different ways. It is the power of prayer that can connect all races and all nations. If we all prayed for a common outcome, it could have a resounding impact on all mankind. After all, what is prayer but a belief in something which we cannot see or touch, but an inner connection with a power which is greater than the sum of all mankind?

I believe that all our prayers are heard and that one day we will all pray at the same time for the common cause.

You see, every human being wants to be loved. Every human being, no matter what color or race or belief or religion, has a spirit. It is that spirit which makes us all equal. Too long have we conflicted over who is right or which belief is better or more accurate. Too long have we fought to persuade the world that our way is better and the other way is not. Too long have we placed emphasis on our differences and not our commonalities. Our elders teach us that no matter where we come from, no matter what race or background we are from, "Our hearts are all the same color". There is no right or wrong when it comes to beliefs, that there is a place for all beliefs. We all have the capacity to love and be loved, and it is love that will bring us all together. Our combined love could have a profound impact on all nations in this world.

I have made the decision to always give back. I have taken so much throughout my life that I dedicate the rest of my days to being the man I was always meant to be. Life on life terms isn't always easy. This life is riddled with so many challenges and hurdles, that it can be overwhelming at times. But I have come to believe that my world can only be measured by the impact I have left, especially with my loved ones. I am not Incorrigible, and as a matter of fact, I never was.

Anishinabeg Medicine Wheel

Keewatinong - Spirit Keeper of the North
Colour: White
Direction: North
Time of Day: Night
Season: Winter
Stage of Life: Elder
Animal: Deer
Plant Medicine: Sweet Grass
Place: Mind

Sha'ngabi'hanong - Spirit Keeper of the West
Colour: Black
Direction: West
Time of Day: Evening
Season: Autumn
Stage of Life: Adult
Animal: Bear
Plant Medicine: Cedar
Place: Physical

Wabanong - Spirit Keeper of the East
Colour: Yellow
Direction: East
Time of Day: Morning
Season: Spring
Stage of Life: Baby
Animal: Eagle
Plant Medicine: Tobacco
Place: Spirit

Shawanong - Spirit Keeper of the South
Colour: Red
Direction: South
Time of Day: Afternoon
Season: Summer
Stage of Life: Youth
Animal: Coyote
Plant Medicine: Sage
Place: Emotion

Where are you on the medicine wheel?

Think about your life and what may be out of balance.

Are you overcome with emotion, easily hurt or embarrassed by something? Then you have an imbalance with the Red spirit (emotion).

Are you physically tired, in pain or ill? Then you have an imbalance with the Black spirit (physical).

Are you working ridiculously long hours or stressed out by the boss and your co-workers? Then you have an imbalance with the White spirit (mind).

Are you obsessed with finding yourself or spending most of your time on self-help books? Then you have an imbalance with the Yellow spirit (spirit).

How can we seek better balance in our lives?

By bringing the mind, spirit, emotions and the body into balance.

The yellow spirit represents our values, what we believe in, what we hold dear, what we are not willing to compromise. Our values affect the White spirit, our decisions. Our decisions affect the Black spirit, our actions, and how we act to implement the decisions we have made. Our actions affect the Red spirit, our emotions, and how we react to the actions we have taken. Our reactions affect the Yellow spirit, our values, and help us to reconfirm or change what we believe in.

The circle continues in this way for every aspect of our lives.

I WANT YOU BESIDE ME

I don't where I'm going I just know where I want to be
I want to be in your arms, and hold you tenderly
I don't know how to tell you just what I feel inside
But I know I'm gonna miss you tonight

I hear you found a new love well I hope he treats you right
Cause you need someone you can lean on, and someone who'll treat you
right
I don't know how to tell you just how I feel inside
But I know I'm gonna miss you tonight

You never know how what you've lost until it's gone
And now I know how much you mean to me – can't you see
If you come back to me, Ill love you for eternity
And treat you with respect and dignity

I know I've made some big mistakes, please forgive me if you can
Let me try to prove to you that I'm a gentleman
I want to learn how to tell you just how I feel inside
Cause I want you here beside me tonight

And now that we're together I promise this to you
I promise to be faithful and I promise to be true
I'm gonna learn to tell just what I feel inside
Cause I want you here beside me – every night.

Lyrics & Music By;
David Languedoc
"Thunder Voice"

THE SERENITY PRAYER

God grant me the serenity

To accept the things I cannot change

The courage to change the things I can

And the Wisdom to know the difference

Author Unknown

CREATOR I LOVE YOU

"Creator I love you
Creator I care,
Creator you've taught me to love and to share
When I'm feeling lost, alone and scared
Creator I know you are there"